V. Sackville-West's
GARDEN BOOK

D1331705

V. Sackville-West's

Garden Book

A collection taken from
IN YOUR GARDEN
IN YOUR GARDEN AGAIN
MORE FOR YOUR GARDEN
EVEN MORE FOR YOUR GARDEN
by Philippa Nicolson

Futura Publications Limited

An Omega Book

First published in Great Britain in 1968
by Michael Joseph Ltd
First Omega edition published in 1975
by Futura Publications Limited
49 Poland Street, London W1A 2LG
Copyright © Nigel Nicolson 1968

ISBN 0 8600 77152
Printed in Great Britain by
Hazell Watson & Viney Ltd
Aylesbury, Bucks

Futura Publications Limited
49 Poland Street,
London W1A 2LG

Contents

Foreword

This volume is an anthology of an anthology of an anthology, using the word once in its original, horticultural, sense, and twice in its literary sense. V. Sackville-West's own 'collection of flowers' was at Sissinghurst Castle, in the Weald of Kent, and from it she culled the weekly garden article which she contributed to the *Observer* from 1947 to 1961, little more than a year before she died. The article became extremely popular – more than she bargained for, since she would sometimes receive over a hundred letters a week from grateful or indignant readers – and in response to many requests she compiled a selection which was published by Michael Joseph in 1951 under the same title as the articles, *In Your Garden*. The articles continued. So did the demand for their republication. In 1953 followed *In Your Garden Again*; in 1955 *More for Your Garden*; and in 1958 (by this time growing desperate for a title) she published *Even More for Your Garden*.

Of these four volumes the last three have remained in print, but the first has not been available for several years. Rather than reprint the four volumes individually as stocks became exhausted, the present anthology has been made to bring together within two covers extracts from them all.

In general the purpose has been to retain the character both of V. Sackville-West's writing and of her gardening. Both were highly individual. She established with her readers a gentle, bantering relationship, like that of an amateur gardener talking to a friend about their horticultural triumphs and follies – boasting a bit, laughing a bit, grousing a bit, mingling reminiscence with hard advice, and sentiment with something approaching poetry. It was a style very easy to parody, for it was conversational more than literary, and it had all the untidiness and colour of a cottage garden. She would write her weekly article almost without correction, reaching sometimes for a horticultural dictionary to check a name or a date, or for a Shakespeare concordance to check a quotation, but she was rarely stuck for a subject or a new idea, since both emerged out of her daily gardening experience. The week's article might be suggested by the plants at which she had been looking the moment before she went indoors to write it; or, even more directly, by the vase of flowers (and she always had several such vases, all small and filled very selectively) that stood on her writing-table.

Thus the articles had a freshness and immediacy which are not lost by transference to a book a decade or more after they were written. They are re-published under the simple heading of the month (but not the year, which is less relevant) when they originally appeared. They have not been re-grouped under subjects of flowering seasons, for that would have altered their character and purpose. In the depth of winter she would imagine summer; in November she remembered May. She would write about a plant when she first ordered it or seeded it; and then six months later about the same plant when it flowered. The seasons and the species were muddled up week by week; and they remain muddled up in this anthology. For the truth is that in any month one can read happily about any flower, and the twelve chapters of this book seek only to give it a rhythm. It needs an index, and it has been given one.

8

What remains consistent is V. Sackville-West's attitude to gardening itself. She was a romantic, and yet she was very practical; she was experimental, and yet she respected tradition; she was literary, but she wrote from knowledge, not from books. Before she married, she had no interest in flowers. In the fifty years of her married life she had but two gardens of her own – Long Barn, near Sevenoaks, from 1915 to 1930, and Sissinghurst Castle, from 1930 to 1962. The first was the laboratory for the second. She made her mistakes at Long Barn; fewer at Sissinghurst. She never stopped experimenting, but gradually she came to form three or four principles of gardening which the reader will find implicit, and some openly stated, in this book.

The first principle was ruthlessness. You must never retain for a second year what displeased you in the first. It must be eradicated. Secondly, she was the opponent of too much tidiness. Let self-seeded plants grow where they naturally fell; let wild flowers sometimes be allowed to invade the garden; if roses stray over a path, the visitor must duck. But, thirdly, there must be a plan – an architectural plan and a colour plan and a seasonal plan. By architecture she did not mean only the layout of a garden's paths, hedges and walls (for which Harold Nicolson was responsible both at Long Barn and at Sissinghurst), but the relation between one group of plants and another, both in mass and in height. The same with colour. She would cut a flower from one part of the garden and carry it around, trying its colour against other plants already growing there until she satisfied herself that she had found the right combination. After World War II, she created her finest achievement at Sissinghurst, the one-colour gardens – white, purple, and yellow-and-orange. As for seasons, she was content to let parts of

9

the garden lie fallow for most of the year once their moments of exuberance had passed. She never preached that something must always be on show everywhere, but that in each flowering season you must always be able to find something important at its best.

As she was still evolving these ideas throughout the period covered by the *Observer* articles, this book is as much a description of her workshop as the photographs (all taken at Sissinghurst) are of her achievement. The reader can learn, for example, how she first conceived the idea of the white garden (p. 14) and then (p. 118) how it turned out. It is horticultural autobiography. But she was writing for people many of whom had neither her knowledge nor resources. Like a good cookery-book, her descriptions were simplified and her recommendations scaled to suit all pockets. She was interested in the possibilities of suburban gardening, while deploring its habitual unadventurousness; and she could write as sympathetically for gardeners without hired help as she could for the old and even for the crippled. This must be one of the least snobbish of gardening books, though it springs from a highly sophisticated garden. It gives pleasure because it describes pleasure. It is a companionable book, enticing and reassuring by turns.

Philippa Nicolson

Sissinghurst Castle (two miles from Cranbrook, Kent) passed into the ownership of the National Trust in April 1967. It is open to the public every day from the beginning of April until the end of October, from 10 a.m. to 7 p.m.

January

Mid-winter flowers

How precious are the flowers of mid-winter! Not the hot-house things, nor even the forced trusses of lilac, most of which, I understand, come from Holland, but the genuine toughs that for some strange reason elect to display themselves out-of-doors at this time of year. The Winter-sweet opens its yellow star-fish against a wall, and the twisted ribbons of the Wych-hazel are disentangling themselves on their leafless branches. Both of these sweet-scented winter flowerers should qualify for a choice for anyone with a plant-token.

Garrya elliptica is not so often seen, though it has been known in this country since 1818; its nickname, the Tassel Bush, describes it best, for it hangs itself from December onwards with soft grey-green catkins eight or ten inches in length, like bunches of enormous caterpillars among the very dark leaves. Some people think it dismal, but a large bush is an imposing sight if you have the patience to wait for it. It does require patience, for it dislikes being moved and, therefore, must be planted small; also you must insist upon getting a male plant, or there will not be any catkins. The female plant will give you only bunches of black fruits. As it will thrive against a north wall, however, where few other things will thrive, it may well be left there to take its time without occupying the space wanted for something else.

Sweet-briar

Someone has been pleading with me to put in a good word for sweet-briar. I do so most willingly, for a hedge of sweet-briar is one of the most desirable things in any garden.

It is thorny enough to keep out intruders, should it be needed as a boundary protection; in early summer it is as pretty as the dog-rose, with its pale pink single flowers; in autumn it turns itself into a sheer wall of scarlet hips; and on moist muggy evenings after rain the scent is really and truly strong in the ambient air. You do not need to crush a leaf between your fingers to provoke the scent: it swells out towards you of its own accord, as you walk past, like a great sail filling suddenly with a breeze off those Spice Islands which Columbus hoped to find.

These are many virtues to claim, but even so we may add to them. It is the Eglantine of the poets, if you like that touch of romance. True, Milton seems to have confused it with something else, probably the honeysuckle:

> ... through the sweet-briar or the Vine,
> Or the twisted Eglantine. ...

but what does that matter? it is pedantic to be so precise, and we should do better to take a hint from Milton and plant a *mixed* hedge of honeysuckle and sweet-briar, with perhaps an ornamental vine twining amongst them – the purple-leafed vine, *Vitis vinifera purpurea*, would look sumptuous among the red hips in October.

I have never seen a hedge of this composition; but why not? Ideas come to one; and it remains only to put them into practice. The nearest that I have got is to grow the common *Clematis Jackmanii* into my sweet-briar, planting the clematis on the north side of the hedge, where the roots are cool and shaded and the great purple flowers come wriggling through southwards into the sun. It looks fine, and the briar gives the clematis just the twiggy kind of support it needs.

Sweet-briar is a strong grower, but is often blamed for going thin and scraggy towards the roots. I find that you can correct this weakness by planting your hedge in the first instance against a system of post-and-wire, and subsequently tying-in the long shoots to the posts and wire instead of pruning them. Tie the shoots horizontally, or bend them downwards if need be, thus obtaining a thick, dense growth, which well compensates you for the initial trouble of setting up the posts and the wire. They will last for years, and so will the briar.

Amy Robsart, with deep rose flowers, and *Lady Penzance*, with coppery-yellow flowers, are particularly to be recommended.

Gardens of one colour

It is amusing to make one-colour gardens. They need not necessarily be large, and they need not necessarily be enclosed, though the enclosure of a dark hedge is, of course, ideal. Failing this, any secluded corner will do, or even a strip of border running under a wall, perhaps the wall of the house. The site chosen must depend upon the general lay-out, the size of the garden, and the opportunities offered. And if you think that one colour would be monotonous, you can have a two- or even a three-colour, provided the colours are happily married, which is sometimes easier of achievement in the vegetable than in the human world. You can have, for instance, the blues and the purples, or the yellows and the bronzes, with their attendant mauves and orange, respectively. Personal taste alone will dictate what you choose.

For my own part, I am trying to make a grey, green, and white garden. This is an experiment which I ardently hope may be successful, though I doubt it. One's best ideas seldom play up in practice to one's expectations, especially in gardening, where everything looks so well on paper and in the catalogues, but fails so lamentably in fulfilment after you have tucked your plants into the soil. Still, one hopes.

My grey, green, and white garden will have the advantage of a high yew hedge behind it, a wall along one side, a strip of box edging along another side, and a path of old brick along the fourth side. It is, in fact, nothing more than a fairly large bed, which has now been divided into halves by a short path of grey flagstones terminating in a rough wooden seat. When you sit on this seat, you will be turning your backs to the yew hedge, and from there I hope you will survey a low sea of grey clumps of foliage, pierced here and there with tall white flowers. I visualize the white trumpets of dozens of Regale lilies, grown three years ago from seed, coming up through the grey of southernwood and artemisia and cotton-lavender, with grey-and-white edging plants such as *Dianthus* 'Mrs Sinkins' and the silvery mats of *Stachys lanata*, more familiar and so much nicer under its English names of Rabbits' Ears or Saviour's Flannel. There will be white pansies, and white peonies, and white irises with their grey leaves . . . at least, I hope there will be all these things. I don't want to boast in advance about my grey, green, and white garden. It may be a terrible failure. I wanted only to suggest that such experiments are worth trying, and that you can adapt them to your own taste and your own opportunities.

All the same, I cannot help hoping that the great ghostly barn-owl will sweep silently across a pale garden, next summer, in the twilight – the pale garden that I am now planting, under the first flakes of snow.*

A Chinese jasmine

As a rule I try to be practical, recommending only such plants as can be grown with some hope of success by the amateur gardener having no advantage of glass or any similar luxury. For once, however, I would like to introduce a climber which does demand shelter from frost, although it may stand out of doors in its pot happily throughout the summer, and, failing a greenhouse, could be safely preserved in a warm room in winter. To do this, you would have to keep it within reasonable bounds by training it round some hoops of sticks, when it makes the most charming pot-plant imaginable. It is so pretty, it flowers so continuously, and smells so deliciously sweet, that it justifies all this extra trouble.

Its name is *Jasminum polyanthum*, a fairly recent introduction from China where I believe it was discovered by Major Lawrence Johnston, the great gardener and creator of the garden at Hidcote. As it strikes very readily from cuttings a home-grown stock may be raised within a very short time if wanted. To look at, it resembles the familiar white summer-flowering jasmine, *officinale*, but the flowers are larger, the scent twenty times as powerful, and the rosy, pointed buds are so pretty among the dark green leaves as to be like little jewels in themselves. I have a sprig six inches long on my table, today in January, carrying twenty-two buds, so its name *polyanthum*, meaning many-flowered, is

* This is now one of the most famous parts of the garden at Sissinghurst.

manifestly well deserved. On the parent plant, now standing in an unheated glass lean-to, a few flowers are already open, a real boon in January. I hope I have said enough to stir temptation.

In the milder counties it could, of course, be grown out of doors, and I have in fact seen a magnificent specimen reaching as high as the eaves of the house in Major Stern's famous garden, Highdown, near Goring-on-Sea, in Sussex. Here it has the wall to protect it from the north wind, and the sea-air which always means less frost. In Devon or Cornwall, or in some sheltered parts of Somerset, Dorset, and Wales, I imagine that it would grow exuberantly and to a great height. Like all such twining things, it tends to get into a tangle, which, as all gardeners know to their cost, leads to a lot of dead wood in the centre and is plaguy to control. The best way of thwarting this airless, lightless jungle is to train some strong shoots sideways, away from the main stem; otherwise we shall find ourselves with a task like unravelling several milesworth of mad hanks of string.

Climbers

Climbers are among the most useful plants in any garden. They take up little ground space, and they can be employed for many purposes: to clothe a boring fence, to scramble over a dead tree, to frame an archway, to drape a wall, to disguise a shed, or to climb lightly into a pergola. They demand comparatively little attention, once they have taken hold of their support, maybe a yearly pruning or a kindly rescue if they have come adrift in a gale.

The clematis is perhaps as popular as any, despite its distressing addiction to the disease known as *wilt*. Few garden-lovers can resist the splendid midsummer purple of the *Jackmanii* hybrids, but there are other forms to choose from, for instance *C. Spooneri*, an ivory-white with curly edges, or *Armandii Snowdrift*, pure white with pointed, ever-green leaves, or, if you prefer a cloud of smoky blue, *Perle d'azur* and *Jouiniana praecox*. If you would like a yellow, with hanging flowers like tiny Chinese lanterns, try *C. tangutica* Gravetye variety; it may not be very showy, but it has its charm when you stand underneath it and look up into its little golden bells.

The enterprising gardener will, however, want to get away from the more obvious climbers, amongst which the clematis must, I suppose, be included. What about *Akebia quinata* and *Akebia trifoliata*, sometimes listed as *A. lobata*? They are not often seen, but they should be. They are both strong growers, semi-evergreen, with shamrock-like leaves and curiously coloured flowers. The flowers of *A. trifoliata* are brown, and the flowers of *A. quinata* are of a dusty violet, which might best be described by that neglected adjective, *gridelin*. Both kinds are hardy, and in a mild climate or after a hot sunny summer will produce fruits the size of a duck's egg, if you will imagine a duck's egg in plum-colour, with a plum's beautiful bloom before it has got rubbed off in the marketing. These fruits have the ad-vantage that their seeds will germinate 100 per cent if you sow them in a pot; at any rate, that has been my experi-ence.

The Akebias will grow tall if you let them, but if you want something which will never exceed 8 to 10 feet let me recommend *Actinidia Kolomikta* as a plant to set against a wall facing east or west. The small white flowers are insig-nificant and may be disregarded; the beauty lies in the leaves, which are triple-coloured, green and pink and white, so gay and decorative and unusual as to provoke friends and visitors into asking what it is.

Hellebores

It has been asserted that, since we admire flowers chiefly because they are not green, it is natural that green flowers should fail to arouse much enthusiasm. If that allegation be true, then our two native hellebores must be ruled out. But I dispute it. The green rose, *R. viridiflora*, gives me much amusement; and I have always longed to come across a plant of the green primrose. I like green flowers, especially when they are of a bright apple-green as in *Helleborus viridis*, commonly called Bear's Foot, or in *Helleborus foetidus*, the Setterwort, even more commonly and certainly more rudely called the Stinking hellebore, found in beechwoods in company of *Daphne laureola* and the Dog's Mercury spurge. Besides, I like any plant that will surprise me out of doors with flowers in January or February.

Perhaps it may soften prejudiced hearts if I add that the hellebores belong to the same botanical family as the buttercups, the *Ranunculaceae*. Few of the English – a most sentimental race – can resist the appeal of the buttercup and those gold-besprent meadows of childhood, and the King-cups growing along the banks of a stream.

Our two native hellebores are becoming rare now, so if you have the luck to find them growing wild in the chalky soil of the South Downland country, please do not dig them up, but make a note to order plants or seeds from a nursery-man or seedsman. Seeds germinate quickly when they are freshly harvested. It is said that ants distribute them in Nature: but as we cannot rely on an obliging ant-heap it is better to buy a packet of fresh seed and sow it at once in a seed box and prick out the plantlings later in the usual way.

I will not contend that either of our two natives is as handsome a plant as the Corsican cousin, *Helleborus corsicus*, so strong and stout that its leaves alone have an architectural quality in the same sense as the Acanthus has an architectural or sculptural quality, quite apart from the beauty and value of the flowers. But I do contend that our two natives are worth adding to any collection of the hellebores. They are humble, and make few demands. They will put up with a considerable amount of shade, and they do not mind lime, in fact they like it, two considerations that ought to appeal to people with difficult patches in their gardens.

Do not be alarmed if *H. viridis* dies away in autumn; it is not dead, it is resting, and will revive. *H. foetidus*, on the contrary, is evergreen.

Rose-leaves

There are certain roses whose charm lies in their foliage as much as in their flowers. They are the roses whose foliage one can describe only by calling it fern-like; and by that I do not mean the ferns of woodland or damp places, but the so-called Maidenhair fern which used to be grown in company of smilax for the decoration of dinner tables at public banquets, and perhaps, for all I know, still is.

First among these tiny-leaved roses I would put *Rosa Farreri persetosa*, otherwise known as the Threepenny-bit rose. It could not be better named, for its bright pink flower is no larger than the old silver thrup'ny bit we seldom have in our pockets or purses now, since it has been replaced by a solid twelve-sided coin of a baser metal. I am told that in Burma it is known as the four-anna bit rose. The Thrup'ny-bit rose is a rare darling, a tiny treasure; not tiny as to growth, for it will go up to six or seven feet high; but tiny as to its leaves and its flock of miniature flowers in early summer. It comes from the South Kansu province of China, growing wild in the Ta-tung Alps, where it was found by Reginald Farrer in 1914. It is perfectly hardy, and renews its prettiness in autumn with small red fruits and colouring leaves.

Other small-leaved roses, all of which will make a big loose shrubby bush, are *Hugonis* and *cantabridgensis*, smothered with butter-yellow flowers in May; *Rosa primula*, yellow; *Rosa rubrifolia*, whose beauty lies chiefly in the contrast between the grey-green leaves and stems the colour of a Victoria plum; *Rosa Willmottiae*, pale pink, usually the first of all to flower and valuable on that score alone, but with the tiresome fault of making an exaggerated amount of dead twiggy wood armed with real little savages of thorns when one goes to clear it out for its own advantage. *Rosa Omeiensis*, white-flowered, has ferocious blood-red thorns, half an inch long, magnificent when the rising or setting sun strikes through them, so take the hint and plant this rose where it will catch the morning or the evening light.

There are other roses which may be chosen for their delicate foliage, their wildly generous growth, and their willingness to fill an otherwise wasted corner. I meant simply to give an indication of what can be found by the intelligent gardener looking through the descriptive catalogues issued by nurserymen who specialize in roses other then the well-known hybrid teas and ramblers.

May I add to correct what seems to be a misapprehension on the part of many people, that roses can still safely be planted up to the beginning or middle of March.

In defence of the lobelia

I should like to put in a good word for the lobelia, dear to the heart of some suburban and most municipal gardeners, but despised by those who pride themselves on a more advanced taste. The poor lobelia has suffered terribly and most unjustly from its traditional use and from association. Association has been the worst enemy of many plants. I suppose that the first time anybody saw pink tulips coming up through forget-me-nots they may have exclaimed in delight. Similarly, the Victorian-Edwardian combination of lobelia and sweet alyssum may once have given pleasure. No longer now.

But can you discard all your preconceived ideas and think of the lobelia as though you had never seen it before? What a fine blue, as good as a gentian, it is not? And so dense, so compact, such a rug, such a closely-woven carpet, you could put a pin though not a finger into the mat of flower. Think of it in this way, and you will instantly begin to see it in a different light and full of different possibilities.

Think of it as a great blue pool. Think of it in terms of waves and washes; think of it in terms of the Mediterranean at its best; think of it in spreads and sweeps, and wapentakes and sokes and bailiwicks and tithings. Or, if you have not quite so much space at your disposal, do at least plant it in really generous patches, not just as an edging, and remember the variety called Cambridge Blue, which lives up to its name.

If you must have it as an edging, and if you must combine it with alyssum, try it with the alyssums called Lilac Queen, Violet Queen, and Royal Carpet, instead of the traditional white. The blue of the lobelia mixes into something very sumptuous with their mauves and purples. And I did observe an amusing and original use of lobelia last summer. The dark blue and the bright blue were planted in neat squares up either side of a narrow path leading from the garden gate to the front door. It was like a slice of chess-board; an Oxford and Cambridge chess-board.

Have I said enough to obtain for lobelia a more kindly treatment? It is such an old friend to our gardens. It came to us two hundred years ago, in 1752, from the Cape of Good Hope, and it received its name in honour of a botanist who worked here much longer ago than that, Mathias de l'Obel, physician to King James I. A romantic story; so romantic that I think our lobelias deserve to be grown with more imagination than is usually vouchsafed them.

The tiny garden

From time to time I get letters from owners of very small gardens, asking what to do about them. These letters usually come from truly keen amateur gardeners, otherwise they would not take the trouble to write. May I quote from a typical letter?

'Our plot is the usual commonplace rectangle, 45 ft. by 175 ft., but I am resolved *not* to have a commonplace garden. Our house stands 40 ft. back from the road, with this pocket-handkerchief frontage ... We hope to plant a camomile lawn, and I have ideas about a lavender hedge ... and we want one or two trees, *not* the usual suburban pink cherry. I thought perhaps the weeping silver lime, *Tilia petiolaris*. ...'

Now this is evidently a gardener after my own heart; and there must be many of them up and down the country. They are restricted as to space, but not restricted in their imaginative ideas. Why, indeed, should anyone have a commonplace garden in the commonplace rectangle? Endless variations are possible, and endless suggestions could be made. For my own part, if I were suddenly required to leave my own garden and to move into a bungalow on a housing estate, or into a council house. I should have no hesitation at all about ruffling the front garden into a wildly unsymmetrical mess and making it as near as possible into a cottage garden, which is probably the prettiest form of gardening ever achieved in this country in its small and unambitious way. I should plant only the best things in it, and only the best forms of the best things, by which I mean that everything should be choice and chosen. When you have only a very small area to your command you cannot afford to be otherwise than selective. Thus, if I had a lawn, it should be of the purest turf; and if I had shrubs they should be specially picked out, the very best lilacs, the very best ceanothus; and if I had bulbs for spring flowering, they should be of the loveliest, most delicate sorts, coming up through clumps of violets smothering the ground; bulbs of Scilla and Chionodoxa and Muscari, the grape-hyacinth, and the dog-tooth violet, and some fritillaries, but always the best and most unusual forms of these; and if I had annuals and biennials to fill up the gaps, they should always be the best, whether they were pansies or carnations.

Naturally, every garden must be a law to itself. So much depends upon soil, aspect, and the taste of the owner. More depends upon his taste than upon his purse. A comforting reflection to end upon.

Rosemary and lavender

Most people cherish a few bushes of these dear, grandmotherly plants. Some people still have the good sense to grow them as hedges either side of a path, or in clumps beside the front-door where you can pinch them as you go in and out. A witty, but rather unkind, remark from a friend of mine, herself a very fine gardener, nearly destroyed my pleasure in the aromatic scent of rosemary. She said it reminded her of Sanitas.

Be that as it may, I shall continue to grow rosemary round my doors.

It occurred to me, however, that there might be some varieties less familiar than the old English lavender, *Lavandula spica*, or the Dutch lavender, *Lavandula vera*, or than the common rosemary, *Rosmarinus officinalis*. Unfortunately, some of them are not quite so hardy, and need protection in winter, but as they all strike very easily from cuttings it is possible to keep a reserve nursery in a frame or under a cloche. The lavender called *Stoechas* is unusual and attractive, rather shorter and stumpier in the flower-spike than most lavenders; it is the one we find growing wild over the stony hills of Mediterranean countries, in Spain and southern France and North Africa. The Hidcote variety of lavender, quite hardy, is very fine: a deep rich purple; and *Twickle Purple* is very similar. As for rosemaries, there is the Corsican one, very beautiful with its feathery foliage and very bright blue flowers, not as hardy as we should like; and there is *Tuscan Blue*, which, as its introducer Mr. Arnold-Forster remarked, is used for hedges in Tuscany where they are 'conspicuous from a distance owing to their ceanothus blue.' His recipe for making it flower well in our country is to shorten the long spikes. I have seen it growing magnificently in Cornwall, trained flat against a wall to a height of quite 10 ft., and I fancy that that would be the safest way to treat it anywhere, save in the mildest climate, with the additional advantage that you could hang some ordinary netting such as one uses to protect fruit buds later on, as a break against frost and wind. It is very stiff and stately, unlike its soft Corsican cousin, with a leathery texture in its dark green leaves, making a handsome plant even if it cannot be induced to flower as luxuriantly as beneath the Italian sun.

Pruning

Argument still rages in the horticultural world about the best time of year to prune roses. According to the old orthodox theory, the time to do it was in the second half of March or in early April. Present-day opinion veers more and more strongly in favour of winter pruning. I don't pretend to be an expert, so please disregard my advice if you disagree with it, but it seems to me common sense to cut the plant when it is dormant, rather than when the sap has begun to rise and must necessarily bleed from the wound.

I know that there are objections. People say 'Oh, but if you prune your roses in December or January, they may start to make fresh growth in the mild weather we sometimes get in late February or early March, and then comes an iron frost and then what happens to those young tender shoots you have encouraged by your precipitate pruning?'

All I can say in answer to that is that you will just have to go over your roses again and cut away all the frost-damaged shoots back to a new eye lower down the stem. You might have to do the same thing after a March pruning, so you will not have lost any time, and on the whole I am on the side of the winter-pruners.

Pruning is such a controversial subject that I approach it with diffidence, but of one thing I am sure: it pays always to clear the dead wood out of any shrub. What a tangled mess accumulates at the base of an old bush of philadelphus! What a lot of useless twigs clutter the lilacs! Take your saw and your secateurs, and give a breathing space, especially in the centre. Let the light in, and the air. This advice is of general application, for there is no shrub that will not benefit. Terrified though we may be of cutting inexpertly into living wood, or of cutting at the wrong time, the most inexperienced amongst us need have no fear in chopping away dead rubbish which Nature herself has discarded. The same applies to those little feeble twiggy growths which will never come to anything and only rob the branch by their small but cumulative filching of the plant's life. Shave them off. Weaklings must be sacrified, in the hard harsh law of Nature.

Wych-hazel

When the early settlers first found themselves self-exiled in that wild and dangerous territory of North America now known to their descendants as Virginia, they discovered in the thickets and undergrowth a shrubby thing that reminded them of the common old hazel they had known in England. They took the forked twigs and used them for dowsing or water-divining, as they had used hazel-twigs at home. This was *Hamamelis virginiana*, and they called it the wych-hazel, because any twig that would twitch in the hand must necessarily have something to do with a witch or a wizard. A pleasing derivation, but our own hazel has no botanical connection with *Hamamelis*, and much as we may appreciate its catkins in spring and the squirrels its nuts in autumn, we must not allow ourselves to be misled.

The wych-hazels we now grow in our gardens are far

better than the one our forefathers found in Virginia. *Hamamelis virginiana* is a very poor thing compared with the Chinese *Hamamelis mollis* or the Japanese *Hamamelis arborea*. These have both been coming into their full beauty since Twelfth Night. They are queer-looking plants with, their twisted growth and their twisted ribbons of flower. One always regrets not having planted more of a thing one likes. This may not be good English, but it is good gardening advice. If I could go back twenty years, I should plant a whole little grove of the two Asiatics, and should now have many large bushes to chop from, instead of being stingy about the few twigs I spare to give my friends. The wych-hazel does not lend itself happily to cutting, which is a pity, for it is ideal as a picked flower, very long-lasting, decorative and capable of scenting a whole room. But it never seems to break out again, as most flowering shrubs do, so when you cut you spoil the chance of next year's shoot. This is the sort of warning that books never give. One has to find out for oneself.

Apart from this drawback, there could be no more accommodating shrub. It may be rather slow of development, but it will start to flower quite young, and will accept any reasonable soil, preferably of a loamy nature. It likes sunlight, to ripen its wood, but will stand up to cold winds even from the north and east, and its flowers are extraordinarily frost-resistant. On winter mornings you can see the crinkled gold coming through the rime like sugared crystallized fruits. If I add to this that in the autumn the leaves turn as yellow as a quince, perhaps I shall have said enough to encourage a wider use of this strangely neglected treasure.

February

Winter-sweet

Chimonanthus fragrans, in English the Winter-sweet, should have a place of honour among plants that will flower out of doors during the winter months. Although it was introduced from China so long ago as 1766, it is not often seen now except in the older gardens, and in honesty I should warn purchasers of young plants that it will not begin to flower until it is five or six years old. But it is worth waiting for. Extremely sweet-scented, even in the cold open air, long sprigs loaded with the strange maroon-and-yellow flowers can be cut all through January and February; it lasts for two or three weeks in water, especially if you smash the stems with a hammer, a hint which applies to all hard-wooded growth. The Winter-sweet will eventually reach to a height of ten feet or more; it is happiest grown against a wall for protection, but I have seen it growing into a big bush in the open in a garden in Kent – not my garden alas!

The text-books instruct us to prune it hard back to the old wood immediately after it has finished flowering; I obediently followed these instructions for years, and got nothing but some truncated little miseries in consequence; then I rebelled, as all good gardeners should rebel when they find their own experience going against the text-book, and left my Winter-sweet unpruned one year, with the rich reward of longer sprays to cut for indoors. I fancy that this extravagant cutting will provide all the pruning that is necessary.

If you are the sort of gardener who likes raising your own nursery stock, leave a couple of sprays to develop their gourd-shaped fruit, and sow the seed when ripe in a pot or pan. It germinates very obligingly.

The Algerian iris

The Algerian iris are most obliging plants, even if mal-treated, but a little extra kindliness and understanding will bring forth an even better response. As is true of most of us, whether plants or humans.

Kindliness, so far as the Algerian iris is concerned, consists in starving it. Rich cultivation makes it run to leaf rather than to flower. What it really enjoys is being grown in a miserably poor soil, mostly composed of old lime and mortar rubble and even gravel: a gritty mixture at the foot of a sunny wall, the grittier and the sunnier the better. Sun and poverty are the two things it likes. To give it the maximum of sun to ripen itself off during the summer, you should chop down its leaves in May or early June and let the sun get at it for so long as our climate allows. There is no more that you can do for it except to guard it against snails and slugs. It is vital to do this if the flower is not to be nibbled and tattered by these creatures, which hibernate so happily within the leaves and in the cracks of the wall. Any proprietary slug-bait will do the job for you, or you can make your own mixture which is far cheaper and just as efficacious with Meta tablets, smashed into a fine powder and mixed with bran, tea-leaves, or even sawdust. It may be unkind to the snails, but one has to make one's choice.

The Algerian iris is known to most of us as *Iris stylosa*. It

29

should, in fact, be called *Iris unguicularis*, because this is the older botanical name for it, *unguiculus* meaning a small or narrow claw. Do we have to bother about that? Let us, rather, record that it is the native of stony ground in Algeria, Greece, Crete, Syria, and Asia Minor, and that it accommodates itself very willingly to our island, flowering before Christmas sometimes, especially after a hot, dry summer, and continuing to flower in mild weather right into March. You should search your clumps of the grass-like leaves every day for possible buds, and pull the promising bud while it still looks like a tiny, tightly-rolled umbrella, and then bring it indoors and watch it open under a lamp. If you have the patience to watch for long enough, you will see this miracle happen.

If you have not yet got this iris in your garden and want to acquire it, you can plant it in March or April; but September is the best time for transplanting. It does not much like being split up and moved, so whenever you acquire it, do make sure that it does not get too dry until it has had time to establish itself. After that, it will give you no trouble.

Tussie-mussies

A dear near neighbour brought me a tussie-mussie this week. The dictionary defines tuzzy-muzzy, or tussie-mussie, as *a bunch or posy of flowers, a nosegay*, and then disobligingly adds that the word is obsolete. I refuse to regard it as obsolete. It is a charming word; I have always used it and shall continue to use it, whatever the great *Oxford Dictionary* may say; and shall now take my neighbour's tussie-mussie as a theme to show what ingenuity, taste, and knowledge can produce from a small garden even in February.

My neighbour has many difficulties to contend with. She is not young, she is into her seventh decade. She has no help in her house. Her garden is wind-swept, and the soil is a stiff Weald of Kent clay. (Only those who have tried to garden on Wealden clay can appreciate what that means.) A jobbing gardener from time to time is all that she commands. She does most of the work herself. Yet she manages to produce a bunch such as I will now describe to you.

It is composed of at least five different flowers, all perfectly chosen. She goes always for the best, which I am sure is the secret of good gardening: choose always the best of any variety you want to grow. Thus, in the bunch she brought me, the violets were *pink* violets, the sort called *Coeur d'Alsace*, and the one *Iris reticulata* she put in was the sort called *Hercules*, which is redder than the familiar purple and gold. The grape-hyacinths were the small sky-blue *azureus*, which flowers earlier and is prettier than the dark blue later sort. The crocus in her bunch was not the common yellow, but had brown markings on its outside; I think it may be *C. susianus* or it may be Moonlight, but I forgot to ask her. The anemone that she put in must be a freakishly early bloom of *Anemone St. Bavo*, amethyst petals with an electric-blue centre. How wise she is to grow *Anemone St. Bavo* instead of the coarser *Anemone St. Brigid*.

The moral of this article, if any newspaper article may have a moral, is that it just shows what you can do if you put your mind to it. I have received many letters saying: 'Do tell us what we can do in a small garden.' My neighbour's tussie-mussie is the answer. She grows those exquisite things in a small, quarter-of-an-acre grassy space under apple trees, and somehow produces a jewelled effect rather like the foreground of Botticelli's *Primavera*. They are all low and brilliant and tiny; and no more difficult to grow than their more ordinary relations.

Rose-hedges

In a gracious, small and ancient town near where I live, someone has had the imagination to plant a hedge of rambler roses. It occupies the whole of his road frontage, about 150 yards I believe, and in the summer months people come from all over the county to see it. I must admit that it is an impressive sight; a blaze of colour; a long, angry, startling streak, as though somebody had taken a red pencil and had scrawled dense red bunches all over a thicket-fence of green. A splendid idea; very effective; but, oh, how crude! I blink on seeing it; and having blinked, I weep. It is not only the virulence of the colour that bring tears to my eyes, but the regret that so fine an idea should not have been more fastidiously carried out.

The hedge is made of *American Pillar*, a rose which, together with *Dorothy Perkins*, should be forever abolished from our gardens. I know this attack on two popular roses will infuriate many people; but if one writes gardening articles one must have the courage of one's opinion. I hate, hate, hate *American Pillar* and her sweetly pink companion *Perkins*. What would I have planted instead? Well, there is *Goldfinch*, an old rambler, very vigorous, very sweet-scented and when I say sweet-scented I mean it, for I do try to tell the exact truth in these articles, not to mislead anybody. *Goldfinch* is a darling; she is my pet, my treasure; a mass of scrambled eggs. Then there is *Félicité et Perpétue*, white, flushed pink; and *Madame Plantier*, white, with larger flowers. Or *Albertine*, very strong and free-flowering, a beautiful soft pink that appears to have been dipped in tea; or *François Juranville* who has also fallen into a tea-cup.

Pergolas

It suddenly occurred to me that I have never written about pergolas, nor am I quite sure that pergolas are altogether suitable for Britain. They drip. Moreover, they are all too often used as a support for the less desirable kinds of rambler rose and their usefulness as a framework for more interesting climbers is often overlooked. Practically all the flowering climbers look fine thus seen overhead, and to them may be added the many sorts of ornamental vine, including the hardy fruiting vines, for what could be prettier than bunches of little grapes dangling, either green or black?

Even the people who prefer to stick exclusively to roses have a wide choice of very beautiful and vigorous varieties. There are old favourites amongst them: *Gloire de Dijon, Lady Hillingdon, Mme Alfred Carrière, William Allen Richardson*; but there are also some loose, huge single or semi-double flowerers: *Allen Chandler*, a blaze of red with gold centres; *Cupid*, a silvery shell-pink; *Emily Gray*, a butter-yellow with shiny dark leaves and reddish stems; and the well-known *Mermaid*, flowering late, a delicate yellow. Many of the favourite hybrid teas may also be had as climbers: *Crimson Glory, Etoile de Hollande, Ophelia, Mme Edouard Herriot*. Then there is *Paul's Lemon Pillar*, one of the most perfectly shaped roses I know, and of so subtle a colour that one does not know whether to call it ivory or sulphur or iceberg green. A very rich yellow is *Lawrence Johnston*, once known as *Hidcote Yellow*; and for a mixture of yellow and red, giving an effect of the most

G.B.—3

brilliant orange, you have *Réveil Dijonnais*, greatly resembling the old Austrian Copper, which, in fact, is one of its
parents, only with far larger flowers. Startling when it first
opens, it has the fault of fading into a truly hideous pinkish
mud.

These are only a very few of the substitutes I would
suggest for my old enemies *American Pillar* and *Dorothy
Perkins*.

Snowdrops

The snowdrops will soon be going over and it is as well to
remember that the time to divide them is immediately after
they have finished flowering, and consequently to plant new
bulbs also in March, if you can induce the bulb merchant to
send them then. It is as well to remember, moreover, that
there are different kinds besides the common snowdrop
(only one hates to call it common). For instance, there is the
finer variety called *Galanthus nivalis viridi-apice*, or green-
tipped; and, of course, there is the double snowdrop, but I
hope nobody would wish to grow that, for surely the whole
beauty lies in the perfection of line of the single bell. Then
there is the tall, large-flowered *Galanthus Elwesii*, from the
hills behind Smyrna, often seen in old cottage gardens but
not so often planted by the modern gardener, a most graceful dangling thing, flowering rather later than the little
Galanthus nivalis, the 'milk-flower of the snow'. For people
who want something really unusual, and are prepared to pay
for it, there is *Galanthus Ikariae*, which has the romantic
peculiarity of growing in a wild state in only one place in
the world: the small island of Ikaria or Nikaria in the
Aegean sea, where Hercules buried the ill-fated Icarus. It
flowers in March, and much resembles the common snow-

drop, except that the flower is a little larger and the leaves curl over backwards.

This by no means exhausts the list (there are fourteen different species), but if anyone should have so perverted a taste as to desire the sight of a snowdrop in autumn, there is *Galanthus Olgae*, which comes from Mount Taygetus, near Sparta, and flowers in October. The leaves come after the flower; and this is a bulb which should positively be planted during the spring months. I fancy that it is the same as *Galanthus octobriensis*, under another name.

Galanthus corcyrensis, from Corfu, flowers in November, and *G. cilicius*, from Syria and Asia Minor, in December.

Crocuses

Children have a gift for asking apparently simple questions to which there is no real answer. I was asked 'What is your favourite flower?' The reply seemed almost to suggest itself: 'Any flower, turn by turn, which happens to be in season at the moment.'

Thus, I now find myself regretting that I did not plant more of the species crocuses which are busy coming out in quick succession. They are so very charming, and so very small. If you can go and see them in a nursery garden or at a flower show, do take the opportunity to make a choice. Grown in bowls or Alpine pans they are enchanting for the house; they recall those miniature works of art created by the great Russian artificer Fabergé in the luxurious days when the very rich could afford such extravagances. Grown in stone troughs out of doors, they look exquisitely in scale with their surroundings, since in open beds or even in pockets of a rockery they are apt to get lost in the vast areas of landscape beyond. One wants to see them close to the eye, fully to appreciate the pencilling on the outside of the petals; it seems to have been drawn with a fine brush, perhaps wielded by some sure-handed Chinese calligrapher, feathering them in bronze or in lilac. Not the least charm of these little crocuses is their habit of throwing up several blooms to a stem (it is claimed for *ancyrensis* that a score will grow from a single bulb). Just when you think they are going off, a fresh crop appears.

Ancyrensis, from Ankara and Asia Minor, yellow, is usually the first to flower in January or early February, closely followed by *chrysanthus* and its seedlings *E. A. Bowles*, yellow and brown; *E. P. Bowles*, a deeper yellow feathered with purple; *Moonlight*, sulphur yellow and cream; *Snow Bunting*, cream and lilac; *Warley White*, feathered with purple. That fine species, *Imperati*, from Naples and Calabria, is slightly larger, violet-blue and straw-coloured; it flowers in February. *Susianus*, February and March, is well known as the Cloth of Gold crocus; *Sieberi*, a Greek, lilac-blue, is also well known; but *Suterianus* and its seedling *Jamie* are less often seen. Jamie must be the tiniest of all: a pale violet with deeper markings on the outside, he is no more than the size of a shilling across when fully expanded, and two inches high. I measured.

I have mentioned only a few of this delightful family, which should, by the way, be planted in August.

Last-hour planting

People don't always realize that there is time up to the middle or even the end of March to do some last-hour planting of trees and shrubs, provided you can get them in when the ground is neither frosty nor waterlogged. We might reasonably hope for a suitable interlude between mid-

February and mid-March, and may I remind you that a shovelful of peat chucked into the hole, and well worked in amongst the fibrous roots as you jiggle-joggle the new plant up and down before finally treading it firm, is of enormous value in conserving moisture and in setting up the root system essential to all plant life. This recommendation to use some peat applies not only to the peat-lovers such as azaleas, *eucryphias*, rhododendrons, Kalmias, and all the ericaceous family of heaths and heathers, but also to things you would not think of, such as roses. Some plants hate lime, but very few plants hate peat.

A handful of bonemeal is also helpful.

These reflections on last-hour planting led me to remember a small, upright deciduous tree. A native of North China, it is called *Xanthoceras sorbifolium*, and it is not my fault if I cannot supply a simpler name in the vernacular. Its habit of upright growth recommends it for small gardens where space is limited, and in May it is a very pretty sight with its many panicles of white flowers rising in stiff vertical terminals amongst the soft green. Related to the horse-chestnut, it is perfectly hardy though a little shelter is perhaps advisable as a protection for the flowers against late frosts; if frost is feared, the flower trusses may be picked, as they lend themselves willingly to indoor forcing.

The spring Snowflake, *Leucojum vernum*, which started coming into flower at the beginning of this month, is worth noticing now with a view to future bulb orders. It is one of those things which repay looking closely into, turning its white, green-tipped bell upwards, as you might turn a child's face upwards by putting your finger under its chin. Any right-minded child would resent and resist; the Snowflake has no option. You may then peer into the delicacy of its structure and its markings, always the best way to appreciate the tinies of drooping habit. Not that the Snowflake fails to make its own little effect in the garden. It accompanies the snowdrops and the aconites, and thus is welcome on a dreary morning when every harbinger and prophet means the beginning of spring.

Practical note: plant the bulbs early, in September. Do not be disappointed if for the first year they do not do much. They need a year to settle down; so, obviously, you must never disturb them again once you have got them established. They like a bit of shade, so are useful to fill up a shady corner where other bulbs might not flourish.

Annuals

Annuals for sunny places are for the most part so well known and so widely grown that it would be almost an insult to list them, and a waste of space to remind you of such things as clarkia, alyssum, candytuft, eschscholtzia, petunia, or even nemesia which certainly gives the highest value for brilliance of colour. Any seedsman's catalogue will gladly propel your memory in the direction of the obvious.

It might therefore be more useful if I were to single out a few which, although quite as easy to grow, seem to have remained oddly bashful with a dislike of publicity. I never tire of recommending *Phacelia campanularia*, and never cease to be surprised when visitors to my garden ask me what it is. Try it. Sow it at intervals of a fortnight from April onwards; put down slug-bait; thin it out to 6 in. apart; and then see what you think of it. Sheets of blue. Then there are the South Africans: *Venidium, Ursinia, Dimorphotheca*, all in the range of yellow to orange; and if you want to increase the orange touch on the palette of your border, there is *Cosmea Orange Ruffles*, 3 ft. tall, feathery of leaf, starry of flower, long-lasting, and pretty enough in a mixed bunch to please even Mrs. Constance Spry. At the foot of all these yellow-to-orange things, you might sow a vast patch of *Limnanthes Douglasii*, beloved of bees, and more descriptively known as the poached-egg flower. I should not have called it poached egg myself: I should have called it scrambled egg with chopped parsley; poached suggests something far more circular and cohesive. I know this is a very ordinary annual to recommend, but one does so easily forget old favourites that a reminder may be forgiven.

Looking back on what I have just written, I see I said sow a vast patch. I am sure this is good and sound advice. Always exaggerate rather than stint. Masses are more effective than mingies.

To conclude. Have you grown *Molucella laevis*? It was introduced into this country from Syria in 1570, over 400 years ago, and seems to have been somewhat neglected until a recent revival of its popularity. I tried it and was disappointed when it first came up; then, as it developed, I saw that it did deserve its other name, the Shell-flower, and from being disappointed I came round to an affection for it. One must be patient with it, for it takes some leisurely summer weeks before it shows what it intends to do.

I was given to understand that it could be picked and kept in a vase indoors throughout the winter, but alas the ruthless hoe came along before I had time to arrest it, and my Shell-flower got carted off to the rubbish heap.

Annuals for rock-gardens

Annuals for rock-gardens? This is surely a suggestion calculated to horrify anyone who regards a rock-garden as a sanctuary for alpine plants expertly set in specially composed pockets between rock and rock, according to their demands of sun or shade, north or south aspect, scree or peat, moisture or drainage. I respect these purists, and should like nothing better than to emulate them. One must, however, consider the case of the humbler amateur, whose ledges and crevices might look sadly bare without the help of those useful little packages of seed.

I would make a condition that any annuals thus admitted should be suitable in scale and in character. The point is perhaps not worth emphasizing, for it would be a duffer of a gardener who introduced heavy solid flowers such as snapdragons amongst the small delicacies of his alpines. The maximum height should not exceed the few inches of *Phacelia*, for example, with a comparably light habit of growth. *Leptosiphon*, now called *Gilia hybrida*, is as feathery as asparagus fern and as parti-coloured as confetti. The tiny *Trachelium*, a mist of blue, although strictly speaking a perennial, is best grown as an annual because it is not quite hardy. The inch-high forget-me-not, *Myosotis alpestris*, and the alpine poppy, *Papaver alpinum*, 2 or 3 in., although not true annuals, may be treated as such, for they will flower the first season even if they do not survive many winters. *Linaria flava*, or *Antirrhinum pumilum*, is a true annual from the Mediterranean, very graceful and pretty, especially if allowed enough space to expand into a little bushlet. Smallest of all, with the longest name, is *Ionopsidium acaule* from Portugal, the Violet cress or diamond flower, which sows itself freely in tufts in odd corners and between the cracks of paving. Anything but ostentatious, it provides a miniature surprise for peering eyes. Wee, cowering and timorous, it prefers to hide itself within the veil of slight shade.

In contrast, the *Portulaca*, rightly called the Sun-plant, may be grown as a carpeter in the driest, grittiest pocket available, and so may *Mesembryanthemum criniflorum*, the Livingstone daisy. Both of these astonish with the harlequin of their colouring. They creep, crawl and kindle whenever the sun coaxes them open. With twilight they fold themselves up for the night, nor will they make much of a showing on a cloudy day. In spite of this drawback I would not be without them, for the proportion of sunny hours in our summer is perhaps greater than our national grumpiness would like us to believe.

Winter-gardening

That frail and lovely little gladiolus *Colvillei* 'The Bride' should have been potted up before Christmas, but it is not too late to do so now. If I had a stony, sun-baked terrace on the Riviera I should grow it by the hundred; as it is, I content myself with a dozen in two pots under glass. I know very well that people do grow it out of doors in England, lifting the corms each autumn as you would do with other gladioli, but its white delicacy is really seen to better advantage as a picked flower than lost in the competition of the garden.

Some gardeners have a theory that the corms are not worth keeping after the first year and that it is better to renew annually. I believe this to be an unnecessarily extravagant idea. The little offsets always to be found clustering round the parent corm may be grown on until they come to flowering size in their second year. Naturally, this means a preliminary gap of one season, but once the rhythm is established the succession is assured. I have found that the same system works with *Acidanthera bicolor Murieliae*, itself a form of gladiolus, and with those tiny starry narcissi *Watereri*, which are difficult to keep otherwise and rather expensive to buy. These, by the way, are a real treasure for a pan in an Alpine house, or in a raised trough out of doors where they can be examined at leisure and more or less at eye-level.

An easier treasure on a staging under glass is the winter aconite. I somewhat nervously lifted a few clumps from the garden just as they were beginning to hump themselves in their round-shouldered way through the ground before the snow came, and transferred them with a fat ball of soil into a couple of low pans. They do not seem to have minded in the least, and are flowering like little suns, a gay sight on a winter morning. It is remarkable how frost-resistant their soft petals are. There is no heating in that greenhouse, and the pans are frozen solid, yet the golden petals remain untouched and I know that when the snow has cleared away, their garden companions will flaunt regardless of how many degrees may follow after the disappearance of the warm white blanket.

March

Christmas and Lenten Roses

There are several kinds of Hellebore, but the two varieties usually seen in English gardens are more familiar under their prettier names of Christmas rose and Lenten rose, *Helleborus niger* and *Helleborus orientalis* respectively. Why the Christmas rose, which is white, should be called black in Latin I could not imagine until I discovered that the adjective referred to the root; but I still cannot imagine why people do not grow both these varieties more freely. They will fill up many an odd corner; their demands are few; and they will give flowers at a time of year when flowers are scarce.

As for their demands, they like a cool place, say a west aspect or a niche shaded by shrubs; a fairly heavy soil, and if it is moist so much the better; the one thing they will not stand is a poor sandy soil which gets dried out in the summer. They do not like being disturbed either, so plant them where you intend them to remain. If you buy plants you will have to wait a couple of years before they do anything very much about flowering, but once established they will improve steadily, especially if you give them an occasional mulch of compost, leaf-mould, or rotted manure.

It is, of course, cheaper to grow them from seed than to buy plants, and the seed germinates very readily if it is freshly harvested, say from the garden of a friend, in May or June.

Both the Christmas and the Lenten roses are true to their association with the calendar, which means that from

December to April the clumps of one or the other are in flower. The Christmas rose is ideal for picking, lasting for weeks indoors if you split the stems. Cover the clump with a hand-light, to avoid splashing with mud from heavy rain. The Lenten rose, alas, is unreliable as a cut flower; sometimes, by splitting the stems, it can be induced to hold up its lovely wine-coloured head for a few days, but at other times under the same treatment it flops mournfully after a few hours; I have never made out why.*

Looking after cyclamen

A pot of cyclamen is a favourite Christmas present, and very nice, too, but by this time (March) some recipients may be wondering what to do with it. Don't throw it away. It will repeat its beauty for you year after year if you treat it right. Treating it right means (1) keeping it moist so long as it continues to flower and to carry leaves; (2) letting it dry off by degrees after the last buds have opened and faded away; (3) keeping it, still in its pot, *unwatered*, in a frost-proof place during the remaining cold weeks, and then standing it out of doors, still unwatered, still in its pot, throughout the spring and early summer in a shady place; (4) starting it into life again in July or August. Starting it into life again merely means giving it water again – very simple. It will then begin, quite quickly, to show new buds all over the corm; but to get the best out of it you ought then to re-pot it. It likes a rather loose soil, made up of fibrous loam, some gritty sand, and a handful of bonemeal, all mixed well together. *Do not bury the corm*; it should sit on top, three-quarters visible. Do not water too much at first,

* Subsequent information: plunge the tips of the stalks into nearly-boiling water.

water more generously when autumn comes and you bring your pots into the shelter of a warm greenhouse if you have one; or on to a warm window-sill if you have not.

Do not ever, at any time, give too much water. If you do, your plant will very quickly notify you by turning its leaves yellow and by developing a soft rot in the stems of the flowers. There seem to be two schools of thought about the best way to water. Some growers say it is better to avoid overhead watering which may cause the corm to rot, and that it is better to stand the pot in a saucer or bowl with an inch or so of water, thus absorbing the moisture through the porous pot up into the roots, remembering to empty the water away when you think the plant has had enough. Other growers condemn the saucer idea.

A cottage friend of mine who grows some superb cyclamen on her kitchen window-sill tells me that her grandmother advised her to water them with weak tea. This may sound like an old wife's tale, but the tales of some old wives sometimes turn out to be right.

There are two kinds of cyclamen: the Persian, which is the one your friends give you, and which is not hardy, and the small, out-door one, a tiny edition of the big Persian, as hardy as a snowdrop. These little cyclamen are among the longest-lived of garden plants. A cyclamen corm will keep itself going for more years than its owner is likely to live. They have other advantages: (1) they will grow under trees, for they tolerate, and indeed enjoy, shade; (2) they do not object to a limy soil; (3) they will seed themselves and (4) they will take you round the calendar by a judicious planting of different sorts. *C. neapolitanum*, for instance, will precede its ivy-like leaves by its little pink flower in late autumn, white flowers if you get the variety *album*;

45

C. coum, pink, white, or lilac, will flower from December to March; *C. ibericum* from February to the end of March; *C. balearicum* will then carry on, followed by *C. repandum*, which takes you into the summer; and, finally, *C. europæum* for the late summer and early autumn. Some botanists believe this to be a native; it was certainly recorded here in the reign of Queen Elizabeth, when, if beaten into little flat cakes, it was considered 'a good amorous medicine to make one in love.'

An unconventional greenhouse

Successful gardening is not necessarily a question of wealth. It is a question of love, taste, and knowledge. There are two things I should like to describe to you in connection with a neighbour of mine, who has fingers so green that the water must surely turn emerald every time she washes her hands. One is the way she has designed her garden, and the other is the way she makes use of her small greenhouse.

Which shall I take first? The greenhouse, perhaps, since this is the time of the year when one can make the best use of a greenhouse for growing seeds and for producing a display of flowers. My neighbour does both, and does it in the most unconventional fashion. It would make any professional gardener laugh, and would send him away scratching his head with a lot to think over. She does the oddest things. She digs up clumps of violets from her outdoor garden and has them blooming exuberantly in pots, the small pink violet and the little almost-blue one; and as she takes the trouble to whitewash her pots, instead of leaving them to their normal hideous terra-cotta colour, you may imagine how the flowers gain in beauty as they pour over those blanched containers, white and clean as blancoed tennis-shoes. She digs up clumps of snowdrops and crocuses, and packs them into an ordinary pudding basin. One end of the house is all flowers and colour; the side-stagings are devoted to seed boxes.

She has not many real wooden seed boxes. There are cardboard dress-boxes tied round with string to prevent them from disintegrating, and old Golden Syrup tins, and even some of those tall tins that once contained Slug-death, and some of those little square chip-baskets called punnets. I verily believe that she would use an old shoe if it came handy. In this curious assortment of receptacles an equally curious assortment of seedlings are coming up, green as a lawn, prolific as mustard-and-cress on a child's bit of flannel. There are cabbages and lettuces in some of them; rare lilies in others; and I noted a terrified little crop of auriculas scurrying up, as though afraid that they might be late for a pricking-out into the warm earth of May.

It all goes to show what you can do if you try, in gardening. There are such possibilities, not necessarily expensive.

I was half mistaken, by the way, in describing this greenhouse as unheated. It *is* unheated as a rule, but on a chilly evening when a threat of frost is in the air an electric tube underneath the staging can be turned on by means of a switch located in the kitchen. What could be simpler? It is rather an extravagant method. But it is clean and labour-saving.

Designing a small garden

The small garden may be a bungalow garden, or a council-house garden, or the garden round an old cottage, or the garden round a new house on a main bus route. In most cases the design will be dictated by the shape of the patch, and by the position of the dwelling-house in it. I would like to suggest a little ingenuity to vary the ordinary pattern.

I have three gardens in mind. One of them has been constructed in front of a small house facing the road. It has been turned into a landscape garden on a miniature scale. The path does not run straight from the front gate to the front door but wanders round sideways, and the middle part of the front garden is occupied by a deep pool surrounded by weeping willows and *Iris sibirica*, reflecting their pale mauve and their deep purple into the water. Some Irish yews have also been planted; and they now reflect their images into the pool, duplicating themselves in the watery mirror and making this tiny garden look twice the size it is.

My next garden also faces a road, a main road. It would have been easy, and obvious, to turn this into a conventional sort of garden. But the owners have designed it cleverly: they have put it sideways to the house, so that the flower beds, which ought in the conventional way, to be geometrically set along the house, are put in a surprising way alongside.

My third garden is the sort of garden I like best. It is a cottage-garden of the best sort, kept by a true gardener. This is a garden that slopes rather vaguely downhill towards Romney Marsh, with views of the Marsh beyond it. It is packed with flowers at all times of the year, so exquisitely arranged that they gain their full value wherever they are. I remember specially a planting of the blue primrose mixed with the blue scilla round the base of a grey stone well-head, a perfectly-chosen combination.

Dog's-tooth violets

The Dog's-tooth violets (*Erythronium dens-canis*) should now be coming into flower, so this is the time to study these curly objects and to decide if you would like to order some for planting next autumn. There will probably be a fine display of them at the Royal Horticultural Society's fortnightly spring shows when anybody living within reach of Vincent Square, Westminster, can go and spend an hour of pure delight at this débutante festival. Of course one must expect everything to look better at a show than it will ever look in one's own garden. The exhibitors have chosen their best specimens, and have arranged them in a very becoming bed of moist dark-brown-velvet peat, showing them up to their best advantage.

The Dog's-tooth violets should be there, beneath the great flowering cherries and almonds of the spring. They are small, they are low, they are humble in stature, not more than six inches high, but with their beautifully mottled leaves and reflexed petals like tiny martagon lilies they are more than worthy of their place. Some of them are natives of central Europe, some of North America; they belong to the lily family and have nothing to do with violets. 'Dog's-tooth' is because of the tuber, which is white and pointed, like a fang. They prefer a little shade; light woodland is ideal for them; they like some sand and peat or leaf mould in their soil, which should be moist but never waterlogged; they dislike being moved, so leave them alone for years once they have settled down. I have seen them flourishing and increasing even under beech-trees, where few things will grow. You can get them in white, pink, purple, and yellow.

The trilliums, or North American wood-lily, also called the Trinity Flower from its triangular shape, flower a little later but enjoy the same conditions of shade and soil. One does not very often see them, but I notice that they always attract attention. Claret-coloured or white, they grow to about a foot high and have the advantage of lasting a very long time, which seems to be true of most woodland things, I suppose because they do not get burnt up by a hot sun. Unfortunately the trilliums are rather expensive, at 3s. 6d. each according to my catalogues; but as they are very striking, a group of only three or four makes quite an effect, and after all one can always add a couple every year. They, as well as the Dog's-tooth violets, are ideal not only for woodland planting but also for a cool shaded place in a rock garden.

The claret-coloured one is *Trillium erectum*. The white one is *Trillium grandiflorum*, which in its native home is known as Wake Robin, a name we commonly give to our wild arum or Lords-and-Ladies.

Waterside plants

In choosing plants for the waterside, I think it is important to remember that their beauty will be doubled if you can arrange for them to be reflected in the water. If the water is covered by floating plants, such as water-lilies, this will not be possible, though one can usually contrive to keep a bare zone round the outside to serve as a mirror. Much will depend, of course, on whether the pond has banked-up sides, or fades away into a swampy level; these are differences which can only be considered on the spot.

For the marshy swamp I would suggest a drift of the moisture-loving primulas; *sikkimensis*, *Florindae*, *japonica*, *chionantha*, *Bulleyana*, *helodoxa*, known as the Glory of the Marsh. If economy is a consideration, as it usually is, these primulas are all easily raised from seed. The tall clematis-like Japanese irises, *I. Kaempferi*, look most beautiful growing amongst them, but I always think their requirements are a little awkward to manage – wet in summer, dry in winter. Nature's water supply usually works the other way round. The blue *Iris laevigata*, on the other hand, does not mind boggy conditions all the year through. *Iris sibirica*, less large and handsome than the Japanese, is exceedingly graceful and pretty and most accommodating, though it does not like being too deeply drowned. *Iris Delavayi* resembles it, and is useful because it flowers later, when *sibirica* is over. The richer the soil, the better for all these irises, even to a mulch of rotted manure.

These are all tall-growing, but if you can spare a special corner, marking it off with a ring of rough stones, do try the little almost-black gold-veined *I. chrysographes*, a real gem; and *I. fulva*, a coppery-red.

Tigridias and gladioli

March is the month for planting tigridias and gladioli. They are both surprisingly cheap for the effect they make, and I will boldly go counter against the book-rules and say that it is worth taking the chance of leaving them in the ground instead of going through that tiresome and time-taking process of digging them up in the autumn, storing them in a frost-proof shed, and replanting them next spring. If you will accept this rash advice, which is not so rash as all that, because it is founded on experiment and experience, I would add that you should bury them deep enough to safeguard them from the top few inches of frozen soil, which is all we get in a normal winter in this country. Of course, you must expect some to fail, but on the whole I have found that a fair proportion will reappear.

Tigridias, the Mexican tiger-flower, should be planted, as many as you can afford, in any narrow, sunny border such as often runs under the south side of the house wall. They are low growing, not a foot in height, and they are of an amazing brilliance and diversity of colour: coral, orange, buttercup-yellow, red, and the purest white. If you have grown them before they will need no recommendation from me. If you have never grown them I beg you to give them a trial; I think you will be surprised.

The gladioli should also be planted this month, or any time at intervals between now and May to get a succession. I am never quite sure what I feel about the gladioli. Handsome, yes; wonderful in colour, yes; helpful for picking, yes; invaluable in the August–September garden, yes; supreme in the late summer flower shows, yes, in those great peacock-tail displays like swords dipped in all the hues of sunrise, sunset and storm. Here I come to a full stop and start saying No. I don't like their habit of fading at the bottom before they have come out at the top. I don't like the top-heaviness which entails staking if you are to avoid a mud-stained flower flattened to the ground. Finally, I don't like the florist-shop look of them. No, take it all round, I cannot love the big gladiolus. It touches not my heart.

The little *Gladiolus primulinus* is a far less massive thing. Not so showy, perhaps, but more delicate to the fastidious taste. They can be had in an astonishing range of colour.

A garden of paving-stones

How much I long sometimes for a courtyard flagged with huge grey paving-stones. I dream of it at night, and I think of it in the daytime, and I make pictures in my mind, and I know with the reasonable part of myself that never in this life shall I achieve such a thing, but still I continue to envy the fortunate people who live in a stone country, such as the Cotswolds, or in the northern counties of Yorkshire, Westmorland, and Cumberland. In this courtyard should grow all kinds of low plants between the flags, encouraged to seed themselves freely ... and just as I had reached this point in my article the post arrived, with a letter asking if I had ever seen a very small garden entirely paved and allowed to become a rug of flowers?

No, I had not, but I had often thought of it, for it seemed a solution to the recurrent problem of the pocket-handkerchief garden, which is all that many people are now able to enjoy. It would be extremely labour-saving: no mowing, no weeds. And very pretty and original. I forsee two objections: the initial cost of the stones, and the fact that most people do like a bit of green grass. There are, however, some elderly or handicapped people to whom the bit of green grass is more of a worry than a pleasure; and as for the cost of the stone, it is possible to use home-made cement blocks which are much cheaper and which in any case would soon get partially covered over. Lakes of aubretia, bumps of thrift, mattresses of yellow stone-crop, hassocks of pinks, rivulets of violets: you see the idea?

Amongst these essential and fundamental coverings I should plant small treasures. Shall we say as an axiom that a very small garden should have very small things in it? The picture should fit the frame. I should have lots of little bulbs, all the spring-flowering bulbs; then for the later months I should let the pale-blue Camassias grow up and some linarias, both pink and purple, such easy things, sowing themselves in every crevice. Every garden-maker should be an artist along his own lines. That is the only possible way to create a garden irrespective, of size or wealth. The tiniest garden is often the loveliest. Look at our cottage gardens, if you need to be convinced.

Camomile lawns

I am often asked about camomile lawns, by people under the mistaken impression that I have got one myself. I did attempt some very unsuccessful little paths, however, which have suffced to show me that camomile hates a shady situation, overhanging trees, and a stodgy soil. The only lawn I have ever seen is in full sun (in the heart of London) and fully lives up to its reputation as a hard-wearing ground cover, harder-wearing than turf, for it gets trampled on by thousands of feet and never seems to show any ill effects. I believe also that it requires mowing less frequently than grass, a great advantage in days when one has to think of avoiding labour.

One sows the seed in drills on a prepared bed; thins out; and transplants the little tufts in due course to the place where they are wanted. They spread fairly rapidly, and the more you squash them flat to the ground the better. The first cutting might have to be done with shears, or at any rate with the blades of a machine set high, because before it has had time to grow into a sward, camomile comes up into wiry stalks and might get easily tugged out altogether. This wiriness disappears after a time, leaving a close plat which by the unobservant would probably be mistaken for an unusually dark green turf. I do not say that camomile has quite the beauty of mown grass, so smooth and fine, green-gold in the sunlight, olive in the long shadows; but for practical purposes it should serve you well.

It goes without saying that the necessary cutting will deprive you of the flowers. They are ugly little things, not to be regretted, unless indeed you wish to make camomile tea or to wash your hair in a decoction or to make an antiseptic lotion which you can do by mixing the flowers with dragon's blood, old swallows' nests, worm-eaten oak, and the fat of a mountain mouse.

Taking cuttings

When writing about propagation I sometimes wonder how many readers find my suggestions intelligible. I imagine that even a schoolchild knows the principles of seed-sowing, but perhaps the instruction to 'take cuttings in the usual way' is not very helpful to those who do not know what the usual way is.

Roughly speaking, there are two kinds of plant which lend themselves to increase by cuttings: the hard-wooded and the soft-wooded. The hard-wooded are the flowering and the evergreen shrubs, such as Forsythia and sweet-bay; roses; and fruit bushes. To take the cuttings, which is best done in September or October, you choose young shoots which have ripened during the summer, and either pull them away from the parent stem with a heel, or cut them off close below one of their own nodes or joints. Anything up to 15 in. is a good length. Take off the lower leaves and the soft unripened tips, set your cuttings upright in a sandy trench which you will previously have prepared with a spade, press them very firmly into the sand, fill in the trench, stamp the soil down, and leave it until the cuttings have formed their roots, when they can safely be transplanted.

This outdoor method is the simplest, as all you need

worry about afterwards is to see that frost has not heaved up the cuttings and loosened them. If you want to be on the safe side, however, you can follow the same procedure in a closed frame, but then you will have to worry about moisture and also about ventilation.

There are a few shrubs which will not root from cuttings, such as magnolias, azaleas, some rhododendrons, camellias, choisyas, some daphnes – all these have to be layered.

Soft-wooded plants which may be increased by cuttings include herbaceous things such as lupins, delphiniums, phlox, which in the spring provide many young shoots from the root. These are best set in pots of sandy compost, and kept in a frame until rooted.

How plants travelled

It is said that some 3,000 years ago Queen Hatshepset sent a fleet to fetch incense-bearing trees from the Land of Punt. These trees, of which thirty-one were successfully transplanted to the temple at Luxor, belonged to the genus *Boswellia*, which produces the resin we still know and use and call frankincense.

These reflections have been induced in me by the fact that I write these words sailing along on precisely the same latitude as the Land of Punt. The story goes to prove that the plant-collecting instinct, or desire to add to the indigenous vegetation of one's own country, is of very ancient origin in man. Sometimes, as in the case of Queen Hatshepset, it has been deliberate and undertaken at considerable expense; sometimes it has been accidental or incidental on some other enterprise, as befell Sir Stamford Raffles when, travelling in the wild mountains of Sumatra in 1818, he had the alarming experience of coming on the hitherto unknown and by far the largest flower in the world. Purple and brick-red in colour, it measured over a yard across, contained a gallon and a half of water, and weighed fifteen pounds. Not without good reason, it received the name *Rafflesia* in his honour. Sometimes, again, one country has acquired the flowers of another through a disaster due to natural causes. Thus bulbs of *Vallota speciosa*, intended for Holland, were cast up on the coast of Yorkshire in or about 1790 with the wreck of a Dutch ship trying to make her way home from the little colony at the foot of Table Mountain. The canny Yorkshiremen picked them up, since when Vallota has always been familiarly known as the Scarborough Lily. *Nerine sarniensis* also, and for the same reason, got itself distributed into northern waters a good way short of its intended destination, for in 1659 it was washed up unnoticed on Guernsey, where to everybody's astonishment it flowered in its natural season a few months later. It was thought to have come from Japan, since the ship had sailed from the Far East; only later was it found growing wild in Cape Province; but it made no difference, for it has always been called the Guernsey Lily.

Planting-out indoor plants

The time has come to plant out bulbs which have flowered in bowls in the house. If this is done regularly every year, it is surprising to see what a collection accumulates in a very short space of time, and how quickly they settle down to their new conditions. It may be true that a strongly forced bulb will not flower again out of doors, until the second season; but as most of us start our bowls in a cool, dark cupboard and bring them into nothing more intense than the warmth of an ordinary living-room, which, in this country, is not saying much, the majority will reappear complete with bud twelve months hence.

It is no good whatsoever trying to preserve the early Roman hyacinth or the paper-white narcissus, but all other hyacinths and all other narcissi (daffodils) lend themselves very obligingly to our wishes. Hyacinths should be planted shallow, with the nose of the bulb only just below soil-level. Narcissus wants to go deeper; and if you are planting in grass, as is the common practice, it is easy to cut three sides of a square of turf, hinge it back, set your bulbs in the hole, hinge the turf into place again and stamp upon it with all the weight of Miss Jekyll's boots.

I treat my bowl-grown bulbs pretty rough. They must take their chance, as I must take mine. They have done their best for me, once, and if only they will repeat even a second-best effort I shall be grateful. The most I do for them is to cut off their spent flowers to save them the effort of seeding, and make them a present of their green leaves necessary to the development of the bulb underground.

April

Plants revive

I must start with a warning not to despair about plants apparently killed by the frosts, ice-rain, east winds, and other afflictions they have had to suffer. They may look dead now, but their powers of revival are astonishing. You may have to cut some shrubs down to ground level, but my recommendations would be not to dig anything up rashly until you are quite, quite certain that it has no intention of putting out green shoots again. This certitude may not come until the summer is well advanced. I remember the agreeable surprises we got after the cruel winter of 1940.

Lavishness in gardens

My liking for gardens to be lavish is an inherent part of my garden philosophy. I like generosity wherever I find it, whether in gardens or elsewhere. I hate to see things scrimp and scrubby. Even the smallest garden can be prodigal within its own limitations, and I would now suggest that you should try the experiment of NOT slaughtering your roses down to almost ground level, at least for this year; and see what happens.

A scented evergreen

A very pleasing little shrub or small tree, not often seen in gardens, has been in flower since the middle of March. It is not at all showy, and most people would pass it by without noticing, unless they happened to catch a whiff of the scent. It is pure vanilla.

This is *Azara microphylla*. I recommend it to gardeners who want something different from the usual, and yet something easy to grow. *Azara microphylla* is quite easy to grow. It is an evergreen; it has neat little shiny leaves that look as though they had been varnished; and it has this tiny yellow flower which is now spreading its scent over my writing table and into the whole of my room. I sit and sniff. Wafts of vanilla come to me as I write.

Azara microphylla is a native of Chile, in South America. Some authorities say that it is not hardy here in Britain except in the favoured climate of Devon or Cornwall. I don't believe this. I have got it thriving where I live in Kent, and I have seen a twenty-foot-high tree of it in the rather colder climate of Gloucestershire. So I would say: plant it and risk it.

It likes to be planted in leaf-mould. It would do well trained on to a wall with a north, or east, or west aspect; by which I mean that the early morning sun would not get at it after a frosty night. This is always an important point to remember when you are planting things affected by frost and by the warm morning sun which comes as too great a shock after the chill of the night. Plants must be let down gently. The transition must not be too quick.

Another shrub I would like to recommend is *Osmanthus Delavayi*. This, also, like the *Azara microphylla*, has dark green box-like leaves and a scented flower, white, not yellow. It flowers in March and April, and you can cut it and cut it, and the more you cut it the better it grows. It is well worth the attention of gardeners who want something away from the ordinary.

How charming they are, and how subtle, these early

spring-flowering shrubs! We are all well accustomed to watching the daffodils come up year by year in the orchard; but how few of us think of fanning our English air with vanilla from *Azara microphylla* or with the scent of the *Osmanthus* which Father Delavay found in Yunnan some sixty years ago.

An anemone

The Pasque-flower, *Anemone Pulsatilla*, is blooming just now, for Easter as its name indicates. This is a native of our Downs, getting rare in its wild state, but still cultivated in gardens. It is a soft and lovely thing, pale lilac in colour with a silvery floss-silk surround: and it can now be obtained also in a rosy-pink colouring, which mixes and merges most exquisitely with the original mauve of the native. It is easy to grow anywhere, though as a native of the chalk hills it appreciates a bed of limy rubble in the sun.

Balsam poplars

The Balsam poplar has now unfolded its very sticky leaf-buds and is scenting the air. It surprises me that this deliciously scented tree should not be more widely grown. It is not too large for even a small garden, and if only our road planners and village beautifiers would plant it in avenues along new roads, or in clumps round our old village greens, every motorist would surely stop with an inquiring sniff. Smells are as difficult to describe as colours, but I should describe this one as a sweet, strong resin, powerful enough to reach for yards around in the open air and almost too strong to put in a vase in your room.

Do not allow yourself to be fobbed off, as I foolishly was, by anyone telling you that *Populus candicans* is as good as

Populus balsamifera. It isn't. You must insist on getting *P. balsamifera*, alternatively known as *tacamahac*, which I take to be a Red Indian name, for the tree is a native of the United States and Canada.

Joys and problems of the clematis

However popular, however ubiquitous, the clematis must remain among the best hardy climbers in our gardens. Consider first their beauty, which may be either flamboyant or delicate. Consider their long flowering period, from April till November. Consider also that they are easy to grow; do not object to lime in the soil; are readily propagated, especially by layering; are very attractive even when not in flower, with their silky-silvery seedheads, which always remind me of Yorkshire terriers curled into a ball; offer an immense variety both of species and hybrids; and may be used in many different ways, for growing over sheds, fences, pergolas, hedges, old trees, or up the walls of houses. The perfect climber? Almost, but there are two snags which worry most people.

There is the problem of pruning. This, I admit, is complicated if you want to go into details, but as a rough working rule it is safe to say that those kinds which flower in the spring and early summer need pruning just after they have flowered, whereas the later flowering kinds (i.e., those that flower on the shoots they have made during the current season) should be pruned in the early spring.

The second worry is *wilt*. You may prefer to call it *Ascochyta Clematidina*, but the result is the same, that your most promising plant will suddenly, without the slightest warning, be discovered hanging like miserable wet string. The cause is known to be a fungus, but the cure, which would be more useful to know, is unknown. The only comfort is that the plant will probably shoot up again from the root; you should, of course, cut the collapsed strands down to the ground to prevent any spread of the disease. It is important also, to obtain plants on their own roots, for they are far less liable to attack.

Slugs, caterpillars, mice, and rabbits are all fond of young clematis, but that is just one of the normal troubles of gardening. Wilt is the real speciality of the clematis.

There is much more to be said about this beautiful plant but space only to say that it likes shade at its roots, and don't let it get too dry.

Currants

The old flowering currant, *Ribes sanguineum*, is a familiar sight in cottage gardens, where it may sometimes be seen clipped into shape as a hedge, and a very dense, pretty hedge it makes, clothed at this time of year with a mass of pink flowers. A most reliable shrub, never taking a year off, and demanding the minimum of care of cultivation, it cannot lay claim to great distinction, and indeed some people despise the somewhat dingy pink of the individual flower; these people, with whom I find myself in agreement, should not be satisfied with the original type, introduced from the west of the United States in 1826, but should obtain its varieties *splendens* and *King Edward VII*, both far brighter in colour and just as accommodating in temperament.

I suppose that most people know the tip of cutting generous sheaves of the common flowering currant in January and putting them in a pail of water indoors, when they will come into flower by March, as purely white as any branch of the wild cherry?

There are, however, other *ribes* less often seen. One of these is *Ribes speciosum*, which I can liken only to a prickly fuchsia. As cross and spiny as a gooseberry, this Californian dangles annually during April and May with quantities of miniature red fuchsia-like flowers, hung in rows of little tassels all along its reddish young shoots. If trained against a wall these shoots will stick out horizontally to a length of 12 or 18 in. with very charming effect, especially if it can be planted where the sunlight will strike the shoots, turning them almost to the blood-red transparency of a garnet or of a dog's pricking ear, backed by a bright light. It is not necessary to give it the protection of a wall, except in very cold districts, for it will grow quite happily as a bush in the open; but there is no doubt that it does make a very decorative wall-covering and you will find that it considerably puzzles people who have never seen it before.

There is also *Ribes aureum*, which I find described in an old catalogue as the Buffalo Currant of the Wild West. The flowers, in this case, are yellow; and have the advantage, for those who like cloves, of diffusing that spicy scent, and there is the further advantage that the leaves in autumn will turn to a fine gold.

Alpine lawns

Once, years ago, I wrote about a thyme lawn I had made, a simple and rather obvious idea which met with a surprising response in popularity, but I don't think I have ever written about an Alpine lawn. Those fortunate people who have walked over the high Alpine pastures of Switzerland or French Savoy or the Austrian Dolomites will know what I mean. In that clean, pure air, fresh as iced water and fluty as a glass of hock, the bright flowers bejewel the turf and cluster up against the natural outcrops of grey rock, edging the quick, narrow rills, silvery as minnows as they trickle from their source: blowing in the mountain breeze and crouching inch-low to the ground in an instinct of self-protection against the mountain gales.

We cannot aspire to so majestic a setting, but in a humble way we can reproduce a patch of Alpine meadow in an English garden. It makes the ideal approach to the little foothills of a rock-garden. The essential thing is to make it as dense as possible; it must be woven, tight as a carpet or a tapestry. Clearly, we cannot use grass as a foundation, unless we are prepared to clip it with nail-scissors, so I suggest some of the close-carpeting plants: the creeping thymes, the little mints, the common yellow stone-crop, the camomile, the blue speedwell, anything which crawls and creeps and mats itself into a green drugget mosaiced in its season by its small gay flowers. If the spring-flowering gentian *acaulis* will grow for you, so much the better; it usually grows all right, forming a thick green mat, even if it does not flower, and a thick green mat is all-important. Again, patches of the silvery *Raoulia australis* are densely matted, but a little apt to take on a moth-eaten appearance. I should not mind some aubretia, discreetly used and not allowed to encroach, nor should I mind some wild violets, reminiscent of the Alpine viola or of our own harebell on the Downs.

The question of moisture is almost bound to arise. Such an underground mesh of little greedy roots will suck every drop from the ground. In the real Alpine meadow there are many small springs, the ground may even be quite spongy, where you may find such things as the magenta saxifrage *oppositifolia*, but such blessings are rare in most parts of England.

A great magnolia

The great white *Magnolia denudata*, or Yulan tree, began to open its flowers along its leafless branches on Easter Saturday, a magnificent sight against the pale blue of the April sky. The cool weather we endured throughout February and March this year suited its arrangements perfectly, for a warm spell during the early months tends to hurry it up, and then the flowers are liable to damage by their two enemies, frost and wind. I wonder that this most lovely of flowering trees is not more often planted. It is of reasonably rapid growth, eventually attaining a height of between twenty and forty feet, and, unlike some of the other magnolias such as *Kobus* and *Campbellii*, has the merit of flowering when still quite young. Any good garden loam suits it, especially if some decayed leaf-mould can be added. It is best planted in April or May, and the vital thing to remember is that it must never be allowed to suffer from drought before it has become established. Once firmly settled into its new home, it can be left to look after itself. Avoid planting it in a frost pocket, or in a position where it will be exposed to the rays of a warm sun after a frosty night: under the lee of a north or west wall is probably the ideal situation, or within the shelter of a shrubbery.

This dignified and comely tree has been known in our gardens since 1789, when it was introduced from China by one of the collectors financed by that enlightened patron of plant-hunters, Sir Joseph Banks. In China it had been known for far longer than that; in fact, for some 1,300 years, growing beside temples and in the garden of the Summer Palace. Presumably it gets caught by frost in its native home also; frost spells ruin to the year's crop of flower, and people who for reasons of limited space feel unwilling to take the risk, in spite of the immense reward in a favourable season, would be better advised to plant the later-flowering *Magnolia Soulangeana*, less pure in its whiteness, for the outside of the petals is stained with pink or purple; or *Magnolia Lennei*, which is frankly rosy, but very beautiful with its huge pink goblets, and seldom suffers from frost unless it has extremely bad luck at the end of April or when those three mischievous ice-saints hold their festival in the middle of May.

An early-flowering shrub

One of the prettiest and easiest of spring-flowering shrubs is surely *Spiræa arguta*, more descriptively known as Bridal Wreath or Foam of May. In a warm season it may well start foaming in April; and foam it does, for every one of its black twiggy growths is smothered tight with innumerable tiny white flowers. In fact you cannot see the plant for the flowers.

It likes a sunny place; is happy in any decent loam; does not object to a slightly calcareous soil; makes a rounded bush about 6 ft. high; and can be increased by layering. There is an earlier one called *Spiræa Thunbergii*, whose leaves are said to colour well in autumn.

Obviously the pure candour of its whiteness would look best against the dark background of a yew hedge, or any dark shrub if yew is not available. I can, however, imagine that it would associate very happily with the Japanese ornamental cherry called *Tai-Haku*, whose huge white petals should unfold at the same time. There comes a moment of twilight when white plants gleam with a peculiar pallor or ghostliness. I dare to say of white, that neutral tint usually regarded as an *absence* of colour, that it is every bit as receptive of changing light as the blues and reds and purples. It may perhaps demand a patiently observing eye, attuned to a subtlety less crude than the strong range of reds and purples that we get in, say, the herbaceous phloxes which miraculously alter their hue as the evening light sinks across them. I love colour, and rejoice in it, but white is lovely to me forever. The ice-green shades that it can take on in certain lights, by twilight or by moonlight, perhaps by moonlight especially, make a dream of the garden, an unreal vision, yet one knows that it isn't unreal at all because one has planted it all for effect.

Planting for effect must include a recommendation of the ornamental cherry *Pandora*. What a lovely thing this is! A puff of cloud, a tuft of tulle. If ever a young tree looked virginal, *Prunus Pandora* emerges from her stem as a *débutante* from her first ball-dress.

Pool gardens

If anybody is thinking of making an ornamental pond, or of improving one already in existence, this is a good time of year to plan it since many water-plants like being planted in May.

Ponds vary in size and in character. Pond is an ugly word; I prefer pool. Pool rhymes with cool, and that is what a pool ought to be, a place to sit by on a summer evening, watching the reflections in the water, and the swallows swooping after the insects on a level flight. It is not possible to lay down rules, since every pool will vary in size, shape, depth and situation, but here at least are a few suggestions.

Water-lilies immediately come to the mind; I suppose everybody knows roughly how to plant these, by setting the roots between two turves, like a sandwich; tying the turves together with strong string, or even placing them in a bit of old sacking and sinking them into a foot or so of water. There is the white one, *candida*, and there are also red ones, *Froebelii* and *fulgens:* a pink one, *liliacea*, and a yellow, *sulphurea*. Then if you do not mind covering the surface of the water, there is the water-hawthorn, *Aponogeton distachyus*, which is very pretty but should perhaps be reserved for a rather larger area than the average pool; and the water-violet, *Hottonia palustris*. Personally I think it a pity to hide the water too much, unless you are anxious to make cover for fish; I like to see clear water in the middle, reflecting the sky and the plants which you will have set round the edge. Of these, we have our native flowering rush, *Butomus umbellatus*, tall and rosy; *Pontederia cordata*, blue; and *Sagitaria*, the arrow-head; these three are indispensable. For a low-growing plant round the margins, the water forget-me-not *Myosotis palustris*, makes a pale blue drift and is an easy spreader. If the pool is large enough, our own native yellow iris is not to be despised; it has the advantage of keeping close into the bank and not walking out into deeper water; but if this is considered too much of a weed, there are the fine Japanese irises, *I. Kaempferi*, with flat clematis-like faces, and the more slender iris *sibirica* which will grow in any moist soil but does not enjoy being permanently water-logged. The same applies to the moisture-loving primulas, but one could go on endlessly thinking of plants for the margin; the difficulty is one of selection, for the choice is varied and wide.

The merits of grit

When we were small, we were constantly being adjured to have more grit. When we grazed our knees falling down on gravel paths, and naturally howled, we were instantly exhorted by an undamaged grown-up not to be such a cry-baby but to show grit, a brief monosyllabic synonym for British fortitude. We thought then, bitterly, that we had got plenty of grit to exhibit in our poor knees already.

If only somebody had given me the same advice in later years when I first embarked on gardening, how grateful I should have been. Grit, grit, lots of grit, the sharper the better. I now believe it to be one of the secrets of good gardening, whether in the potting-shed or in the rock-garden. I got an Easter present (from myself to myself) of 5 cubic yards of this deliciously crumbly stuff, so I now have a heap which I hope will last me for years. The sort to ask for is called $\frac{3}{16}$ths of an inch. Hitherto I had made do with washed silver sand, but this is better.

Mixed in with loam and leaf-mould for potting, it keeps the soil beautifully open; you can squeeze a moist fistful as hard as you like and it will not coagulate. Crocks in the bottom of the pot, an inch-deep layer of sphagnum moss, and the mixture on top, is the recipe. No plant or seedling should damp off, even if you overwater, as in our anxiety we are sometimes apt to do. Then if you want to make up any special bed, say for bulbs that enjoy good drainage, you follow the same procedure by tipping a barrow-load of the grit into the required pocket, stirring it into the soil, and topping it up with an extra scatter of the grit to be washed in by rain. This ought to suit all bulbs that like a good ripening off, such as ixias, many lilies, or the little early irises of the reticulata family, including *I. histrioides* and the green-black *I. tuberosa* whose correct name is *Hermodactylus tuberosus*. I think also that we might be enabled to grow some of that reputedly difficult race, the Regeliocyclus and Onco-cyclus irises . . . but I am getting carried away by the possibilities offered by grit, and must come down with a crash on to a dear, valued, very ordinary winter-flowering thing, *Iris stylosa* (*unguicularis*). I propose to plant this into a bed of pure grit, and see what happens.

One has these good intentions. How seldom one carries them out. There is always something else to do. A gardener should have nine times as many lives as a cat.

May

Lilac

By the time this article appears the lilac should be in flower. It is not called lilac now by the experts: it is called syringa; and what we used to call syringa is now called philadelphus. All very confusing, so let us incorrectly retain the old names for the moment, when everyone will know what I mean.

Lilac (or laylock, if you prefer) is one of the few old favourites which has been definitely improved in recent years. Frankly, the pale mauve type was a washy thing. The newer sorts have gained in colour, size, and scent. I suppose that everyone is by now familiar with the earlier improvements: *Souvenir de Louis Spaeth*, and *Charles Joly*, both dark red; or *Charles X*, deep purple; or *Madame Lemoine*, double white; none of which is easy to beat. But not everyone, I find, is familiar with the more recent hybrids, carrying truly noble plumes of immense weight: *Réaumur*, dark red; *President Poincaré* and *Pasteur*, both claret; *Congo*, very dark reddish-purple; *Jeanne d'Arc*, double white; *Mme F. Morel*, mauvish pink; *Maréchal Foch*, red.

Any lilac is 'easy'; they do not object to lime, in fact they like it; they need no pruning, though it is most advantageous to cut off the faded flowers, *this is really important*; they are perfectly hardy; and very long-lived unless they suddenly die back, which sometimes happens. Of course they repay rich cultivation; most plants do. And they like the sun.

The old syringa or Mock Orange, is another easy-going shrub, too often forgotten. Personally I like the early, very sweet-scented species, called *coronarius*, found in most old gardens; but *Virginal*, with double-flowers, is a lovely cool green-and-white sight in midsummer; and so are *Belle Etoile* and *purpureo-maculatus*, both blotched with maroon in the centre. *Grandiflorus* is the one with big single white flowers, very decorative but entirely scentless, which may be a recommendation for people who do not like heavily-scented flowers in their rooms. By the way, if you strip all the leaves from cut branches of syringa they will last far longer, besides gaining in beauty. Try. And smash the woody stems with a hammer.

A spring afternoon

Agreeable incidents do continue to occur from time to time, and there still seem to be days when things marvellously go right instead of wrong, rarities to be recorded with gratitude before they can be forgotten.

Such a day, culminating in such an incident, was given to me recently. I had had occasion to drive across ten miles of Kent, through the orchard country. The apple-blossom was not yet fully out; and it was still in that fugitive precious stage of being more of a promise than a fulfilment. Apple-blossom too quickly becomes overblown, whereas its true character is to be as tightly youthful as an eighteen-year-old poet. There they were, the closed buds just flushing pink, making a faintly roseate haze over the old trees grey with age; closed buds of youth graciously blushing as youth must blush in the presence of age, knowing very well that within a few months they themselves would turn into the apples of autumnal fruit.

But if the apple-blossom was no more than a pink veil thrown over the orchards, the cherry was at its most magnificent. Never had it looked more lavish, nor so white, so candidly white. This heavy whiteness of the cherry, always enhanced by the contrasting blackness of the branches, was on this particular afternoon deepened – if white may be said to deepen – by a pewter-grey sky of storm as a backcloth; and I thought, not for the first time, how perfectly married were these two effects of April: the dazzling blossom and the peculiarly lurid heaven which is only half a menace. Only half, for however wrathful it may pretend to be overhead, there are gleams of light round the edges, with lances of sun striking a church tower somewhere in the landscape. It is not a true threat; it is a temporary threat, put on for its theatrical effect – Nature's original of that most strange and beautiful of man's new inventions, flood-lighting.

Enriched by these experiences I came home, expecting no further delight that day; but on arrival I saw a closed van at the front door. Having long awaited some spare parts to repair the boiler, dreary, yet necessary, I walked round to the back of the van, thinking how quickly utilitarian life returned to oust beauty, and with a sigh prepared to investigate some graceless assortment of ironmongery whose function would be incomprehensible to me. But there was no such thing. Instead, a smiling young man confronted me, saying he did not know if I would be interested, but he had brought these . . . and opened the van as he spoke.

'These' were giant pansies, thousands and thousands of them. The van's dark interior was a cavern of colour. Some royal hand had flung rugs of velvet over the stacks of wooden trays. Purples were there; and subtler colours than purple: bronze and greenish-yellow and claret and rose-red, all in their queer cat-faces of crumpled velvet. I stood amazed. What an imaginative young man, I thought, to hawk this giant strain round the countryside, selling his plants to any buyer. When I questioned him, he said modestly, that he hoped people would not be able to resist them.

He was probably right, and I wish him good luck in his enterprise. As for those whose houses do not lie on his road, a packet of seed should serve the purpose, and by next spring the ground should appear as though spread with the most sumptuous carpet from Isfahan.

A way to grow clematis

An unusual way of treating clematis is to grow it horizontally instead of vertically. For this, you need a kind of oblong trellis of bamboo sticks, supported at each of the four corners on four stout little posts, about two feet high from the ground; or a rectangle of rabbit wire or sheep wire will do equally well, besides proving more durable. The effect to be aimed at is a low, flat, open-work table top, under which you plant your plant, and allow it to grow up through. Every few days in the growing season, you will have to go round and weave the strands in and out of the wire or trellis, for clematis grows at an amazing rate, once it starts, and its instinct is to grow perpendicularly, not flatly; but do this as gingerly as you can, for clematis seems to resent the touch of the human hand.

Does all this sound too complicated? It isn't really, and the reward is great. For one thing you will be able to gaze right down into the upturned face of the flower instead of having to crane your neck to observe the tangle of colour hanging perhaps ten or twenty feet about your head. The full beauty of the flower is thus exposed to you, in a way that it never is when you see it only from underneath. And for another thing, the clematis itself will get the benefit of shade on its roots, in this case its own shade, with its head in the sun, which is what all clematis enjoy.

The big-flowered *Jackmanii* type is the most suitable for growing like this, or the Patens group, because both these kinds have flat flowers. The well-known dark purple *Jackmanii* looks splendid, or its variety *rubra*. *Nelly Moser* is a pale mauve, with a pink stripe; *Gipsy Queen* a very deep purple.

The same idea could be extended to many other climbers, say Honeysuckle, or the annual Morning Glory, and even to the strong-growing kinds of rose. The hybrid perpetuals, such as *Frau Karl Druschki*, white, or *Ulrich Brunner*, cherry-red, or *Hugh Dickson*, dark red, or the old pink thornless rose, *Zéphyrine Drouhin* (hybrid Bourbon) will break out from every joint if bent over in this way or merely pegged down to the ground at the tip of the shoots. The extra crop of flowers you will thus obtain imposes rather a strain on the plant, so leave only three or four shoots and give a little encouragement with manure or compost.

Sweet Woodruff

Some proverbs are piercingly true; some are not true at all; some are half true. One of the half-true ones is the one that says familiarity breeds contempt.

Contempt is the wrong word. What we really mean is that we take certain virtues for granted when we live with them day by day. Our appreciation becomes blunted, even as the beautifully sharp blade of the pruning-knife someone gave us as a Christmas present has become blunted by Easter. There are things we grow in our gardens and forget about, and then remember suddenly, as I have just remembered the Sweet Woodruff, that meek, lowly, bright green native of Britain, so easy to grow, so rapid in propagation – every little bit of root will grow and extend itself – keeping weeds down and making a bright green strip or patch wherever you want it.

Sweet Woodruff is its pretty English name. *Asperula odorata* is its Latin name.

You can use it in many ways. You can grow it where other plants would not grow, in shade and even under the drip of trees. You can grow it as a covering plant to keep weeds away. Then, in the autumn, you can cut the leaves and dry them and make them into sachets which smell like new-mown grass and have the faculty of retaining their scent for years.

It is not showy. Its little white flowers make no display, but it is a useful carpeter for blank spaces, and it certainly makes 'sweet bags' for hanging in the linen cupboard to discourage the moth or to put under your pillow at night. Take note that is has no scent until it is cut and dried, so do not be disappointed if you walk beside it in the garden and catch no puff of scent as you stroll. Which reminds me that this month of May is the time to sow that small, dim-coloured thing, *Mathiola bicornis*, the night-scented stock. I have just sown half an ounce of it, which cost me no more than 1s. 3d. all along the pathway at the foot of a yew hedge, and now look forward to some warm evening when the pale barn-owl is ranging over the orchard and the strong scent of the little stock surprises me as I go. This is anticipating the summer, when only recently snow lay upon the ground, but this modest little annual is so easily forgotten that a prod of reminder should not come amiss. If you mix the seed with the seed of Virginian stock, you will get a little colour in the daytime as well as the scent after dusk.

Virginia creeper

Snobbishness exists among gardeners, even as it exists among other sections of the community. The gardener's special brand consists in a refusal to grow plants which of, startling beauty in themselves, have become too trite to seem worthy of a place in any self-respecting gardener's garden.

Trite is a sharp, unkind little word. In the dictionary definition it means 'worn out by constant use; devoid of freshness or novelty; hackneyed, commonplace, stale.' I must agree that we all get tired of seeing certain plants all over the place – aubretia, for instance, being allowed to blanket every so-called rock garden; and the Virginia creeper, *Ampelopsis Veitchii*, glued to red-brick houses, where its colour swears horribly with the brick when it turns to flame in autumn. Yet, could we but behold either of these for the first time, we should shout in amazement.

It is too late to hope for such an experience, but I do suggest that much can be achieved by using these poor vulgarized plants in a different way and in the right place. There is, for instance, a big silver birch of my acquaintance into which a Virginia creeper has loosely clambered. When I first saw it I couldn't think what it was. Great swags and festoons of scarlet hung in the sunlight amongst the black and silver branches of the tree, gracefully and gloriously looping from bough to bough, like something (I imagine, perhaps incorrectly) in a tropical forest, or at any rate like a stained-glass window or like glasses of wine held up to the light. It convinced me once and for all that *Ampelopsis Veitchii* should be grown *transparently*, not plastered against

78

a wall. Any tall old tree would serve the purpose, an ancient pear or apple, or a poplar, if you cannot command a silver birch; and I think the same advice would apply to many of the ornamental vines, such as *Vitis Coignetiae*, with its great shield-shaped leaves of pink and gold, or *Vitis purpurea*, whose name explains itself.

Shrub roses

The roses are coming out, and I hope everybody will take the opportunity of seeing as many of the *old* roses as possible. They may roughly be described as roses which should be grown as shrubs; that is, allowed to ramp away into big bushes, and allowed also to travel about underground if they are on their own roots and come up in fine carelessness some yards from the parent plant.

The old roses are a wide subject to embark on. You have to consider the Gallicas, the Damasks, the Centifolias or Cabbage, the Musks, the China, the Rose of Provins . . . all more romantic the one than the other. Take this phrase alone: 'In the twelfth century the dark red Gallic rose was cultivated by the Arabs in Spain with the tradition that it was brought from Persia in the seventh century.' That is pure poetry, surely, although it comes from a serious article in a serious journal and was not intended as anything but a mere statement of fact. It should send us with a new zest in pursuit of these once neglected beauties.

They are not neglected now; their virtues are recognized by professional gardeners and amateur gardeners alike. True, I have heard conventionally-minded people remark that they like a rose to be a rose, by which they apparently mean an overblown pink, scarlet, or yellow object desirable enough in itself, but lacking the subtlety to be found in some of these traditional roses which might well be picked off a medieval tapestry or a piece of Stuart needlework. Indeed, I think you should approach them as though they were textiles rather than flowers. The velvet vermilion of petals, the stamens of quivering gold, the slaty purple of *Cardinal Richelieu*, the loose dark red and gold of *Alain Blanchard*; I could go on for ever, but always I should come back to the idea of embroidery and of velvet and of the damask with which some of them share their name. They have a quality of their own; and from the gardener's point of view they give little trouble. No pruning to speak of, only a yearly removal of dead wood, and some strong stakes which seldom need renewing.

Roots under stones

I have come to the conclusion, after many years of sometimes sad experience, that you cannot come to any conclusion at all. But one simple thing I have discovered in gardening; a simple thing one never sees mentioned in gardening books. It is the fact that many plants do better if they can get their roots under stones.

I am not thinking specially of Alpines whose natural habit it is, but of casual strays, often self-sown, sometimes bulbous plants, sometimes merely annuals or biennials, which by successful accident have pointed the way to this method of gardening. The narrowest crack in a path or paved terrace will surprisingly send up the finest seedling; I have known even such large unwanted subjects as delphiniums and hollyhocks to make the attempt. The reason, obviously, is that they never suffer from either excessive moisture or excessive drought; the stone preserves such moisture as is in the soil, but prevents the soggy puddling consequent on a heavy rainfall; furthermore, it protects from the scorching sun and consequent wilting which demands the water-can.

I should then fill up the cracks with good soil or compost, and sow quite recklessly. I should not mind how ordinary my candidates were, Royal Blue forget-me-not, pansies, wallflowers, Indian pinks, alyssum Violet Queen, because I should pull up 95 per cent later on, leaving only single specimens here and there. It is not, after all, a flower-bed that we are trying to create. If, however, you think it is a waste of opportunity to sow such ordinary things, there are plenty of low-growing plants of a choicer kind, especially those which dislike excessive damp at the root throughout the winter: this covering of stone would protect them from that. The old-fashioned pinks would make charming tufts: *Dad's favourite*, or *Inchmery*, or *Little Jock*, or *Susan*, or *Thomas*. The Allwoodii, with their suggestion of chintz and of patchwork quilts, should also succeed under such conditions; I confess to repeated failures with them in open borders, but their neatness and variety encourage perseverance.

Pot-gardening

The happy few who still maintain a greenhouse, however small, sufficiently warmed in winter to keep the frost out, will find themselves repaid if they can make room for a few pots of the unfamiliar, pretty, blue-flowered *Oxypetalum caeruleum*.* This, admittedly, is subtle rather than showy, but I notice that it always attracts attention when we stand the pots out of doors for the summer in the garden. It has downy-green leaves and flowers of a curious greyish-blue,

---

* *Oxypetalum caeruleum* is now known as *Tweedia caerulea*, or *Amblyopetalum caeruleum*. It is a native of Brazil.

with a bright blue button no bigger than a flattened seed-pearl in the middle. I like to associate it with some pots of *Plumbago capensis*, whose stronger blue marries into a mist of blues reinforcing one another. Both, of course, are cool greenhouse plants, but they will live very happily in the open from the end of May until October.

I like the habit of pot gardening. It reminds me of the South – Italy, Spain, Provence, where pots of carnation and zinnias are stood carelessly about in a sunny courtyard or rising in tiers on the treads of an outside stair, dusty but oh how gay! I know it entails constant watering, but consider the convenience of being able to set down a smear of colour just where you need it, in some corner where an earlier flower has gone off. We should take this hint from other lands. We do not make nearly enough use of pots in our country, partly, I suspect, because we have no tradition of pot-making here, nothing to compare with the camellia-pot, a common thing in Italy, swagged with garlands looped from a lion's mouth.

Meanwhile we surround a huge black Chinese Jar with the blue *Oxypetalum* and the blue plumbago all through the summer, and drop a potful of *Ipomoea rubrocaerulea* (Morning Glory, Heavenly Blue) into the Chinese jar, to pour downwards into a symphony of different blues.

The Chinese jar is of romantic origin. It was made during the Ming dynasty, which might mean anything between 1368 and 1644 – and was used to transport porcelain from China to Egypt, packed in lard to keep it from rattling about. The very solid handles show where the ropes were passed through, to sling it on board ship. It is not really black, but a sort of aubergine colour.

Some irises

Amidst all the pomp and grandeur of the oncoming June *foison*, some charming modest little irises blow almost unperceived. They are *Iris innominata*, *Iris Douglasiana*, *Iris graminea*, and *Iris japonica*. Let me take them in order.

Iris innominata comes from the north-western States of America. It is no more than 6 or 8 in. high, flowering amongst grasslike leaves, and it varies in colour, from a deep buff or a bronze to a pale lilac, dark lilac, a pale pink, a pale buff. A variation full of interest; and an ideal pet for a pocket in the rock-garden. It is not cheap to buy, but can be grown from seed, an experiment which would demand the usual patience but might easily produce some interesting hybrids. It is said to like leaf-mould and sand, a moist position, and semi-shade, I have it growing in ordinary garden soil, bone-dry, in full sun, and it couldn't be flowering more extravagantly. Perhaps it will flower itself to death, but at the moment it shows no such intention.

Iris Douglasiana somewhat resembles it. I have not got it, but I have seen it at shows and elsewhere, when I determined that it was a *must have*. This, again, produces many hybrid forms and can be grown from seed.

Iris graminea I do possess, and grow less for the garden value of its pinky-mauve flowers, almost hidden at the base of the leaf-clump, as for its curious scent, like a sun-warmed greengage. It is essentially a little iris for picking, and can be seen very prettily marked once you have sorted it out from its leaves and can observe it closely in a glass or vase.

Finally, *Iris japonica* always seems to attract attention. Its delicate and much-branched flower stalks rise from amongst truly hideous leaves, the moral being that it should always be planted in an unwanted corner where its untidiness will not matter. Watch, also, for its tiresome habit of heaving its rhizomes out of the ground. As a cut flower it is so lovely that the non-gardener, asked to name it, will probably mistake it for some kind of orchid. A great advantage is that every bud opens in succession, so that its flowering period lasts for weeks. Do not confuse it with the so-called Japanese irises, *Kaempferi*, for it is quite different. Ledger's variety is the best.

Iris pumila and *chamæiris* are well known: we have all grown them for years, and if we haven't we should. I shall not bother you with the botanical differences between the two. For the average gardener they can safely go under the same name. And how pretty and easy they are: stumpy little irises coming up amongst stumpy leaves. They flower so generously, and lend themselves so readily to division and increase of their rhizomes. If you have one, you can make two; and if you have a dozen, you can make two dozen, splitting them up and replanting directly after they have flowered.

What people perhaps don't realize is that there is now available a whole lot of named varieties of these small irises. They go under fancy names: Mist o' pink, The Bride, Amber Queen, Orange Queen, Blue Lagoon, Burgundy, Mauve Mist, and many others, all desirable. They vary in height from 6 to 8 in. *Mist o' Pink* is one of the loveliest; *cyanea*, blue, is scented. I am attracted by the name *The Great Smokies*, described as a smoky red-purple 8 in., but I have never seen it in flower. Sentimentalists may be attracted by *Tiny Treasure*, yellow, 6 in.

There are many places where all these tinies may be grown. On the top of a dry-wall; in the rock-garden; flourishing in troughs or in a flagged path where they seem particularly happy, getting their roots under the cool cover of the stone, or grown on a raised bed where they get the drainage they like. All they ask is a sunny open place and good drainage. Some people like to grow them in a wide band along the front of a border, as an edging, much as you might use pinks or thrift. This arrangement never appeals to me, personally, because I think their small delicacy is lost in conjunction with the stronger oncoming growth of herbaceous plants; to show up to their best, they need an otherwise bare place to themselves. I fancy, however, that they would associate very prettily with some of the miniature or fairy roses; their scale would be in accordance.

This is the time to order and obtain the little irises.

Protection against frost

Our ideas on this subject of hardiness have to be constantly revised. In an old nursery catalogue of nearly a hundred years ago I find *Alstroemeria ligtu* advertised as suitable for the hot-house, and the hardy little *Cyclamen repandum* for the greenhouse. *Alstroemeria aurantiaca*, the common yellow Peruvian lily, long since discarded as too invasive a weed and seldom seen now except in a wild corner or in cottage gardens, is also recommended for the greenhouse. Such misapprehensions make us smile, but I fancy we should not be too superior and should humbly remember that we still have much to learn. I learnt a lot from February 1956, and from previous experiences. I am now convinced that it is as important to wrap the ankles, legs and thighs of woody growth as to protect the shoulders and head with hessian or other covering. Warm gaiters of sacking, bound round with string, may prevent the bark from being torn asunder by frost or the trunk itself from splitting, a fatal injury never to be survived. I would instance an old lemon verbena growing in my garden for many years. This year, for the first time, we covered it entirely; and can I find any sign of life in it? I cannot. It did much better with a heap of ashes over its feet, a gaiter of straw-stuffed sacking up its shins and its top left to take all risks for itself.

On the whole, I think this past winter has been less destructive than the winter of 1946–47. That was the winter when we got the ice-rain, and all our shrubs became coated with ice and turned into frozen beards against the house-wall, or tinkled like glass chandeliers in the open, stirred by the breeze, and the boughs of the trees themselves became iridescent as the low rays of the sun struck them; and the puzzled birds, trying to perch, skidded up and down, finding no claw-hold.

We were spared this in 1956, and I still feel optimistic, even about *Caryopteris clandonensis*, which threatened to desert me for ever, and a ceanothus which would have been a serious loss.

Carpeting the soil

The more I prowl round my garden at this time of year, especially during that stolen hour of half-dusk between tea and supper, the more do I become convinced that a great secret of good gardening lies in covering every patch of the ground with some suitable carpeter. Much as I love the chocolate look of the earth in winter, when spring comes back I always feel that I have not done enough, not nearly enough, to plant up the odd corners with little low things that will crawl about, keep weeds away, and tuck themselves into chinks that would otherwise be devoid of interest or prettiness.

The violets, for instance – I would not despise even our native *Viola odorata* of the banks and hedgerows, either in its blue or its white form, so well deserving the adjective *odorata*. And how it spreads, wherever it is happy, so why not let it roam and range as it listeth? (I defy any foreigner to pronounce that word.) There are other violets, more choice than our wilding; the little pink *Coeur d'Alsace*, or *Viola labradorica*, for instance, which from a few thin roots planted last year is now making huge clumps and bumps of purplish leaf and wine-coloured flower, and is sowing itself all over the place wherever it is wanted or not wanted. It is never not wanted, for it can be lifted and removed to another place, where it will spread at its good will.

There are many other carpeters besides the violets, some for sunny places and some for shade. For sunny places the thymes are perhaps unequalled, but the sunny places are never difficult to fill. Shady corners are more likely to worry the gardener trying to follow my advice of cram, cram, cram every chink and cranny. *Arenaria balearica* loves a dark, damp home, especially if it can be allowed to crawl adhesively over mossy stones. On a dark green mat it produces masses of what must be one of the tinest flowers, pure white, starry; an easy-going jewel for the tight situation. *Cotula squalida* is much nicer than its name: it is like a miniature fern, and it will spread widely and will help to keep the weeds away.

The *Acaenas* will likewise spread widely, and should do well in shade; they have bronzy-coloured leaves and crawl neatly over their territory. The list of carpeters is endless, and I wish I had enough space to amplify these few suggestions. The one thing I feel sure of is that every odd corner should be packed with something permanent, something of interest and beauty, something tucking itself into something else in the natural way of plants when they sow themselves and combine as we never could combine them with all our skill and knowledge.

Euphorbias

There is a family of plants so easy to grow, so diverse in their character and their interest, that I wonder they are not more freely used in our gardens. I mean the great family of the euphorbias, said to contain over one thousand members. The grandest of them is *Euphorbia pulcherrima*, which we know better under the familiar name of poinsettia, but that is not a plant for anybody without a hot greenhouse.

Other euphorbias are for anybody with an ordinary garden. Would it sound less alarming if I called them by their English name, spurge? There are about a dozen native to this island, from the common wood spurge, which is well worth growing in a rough place as a ground cover under trees if you do not fear it as an invader, to the queerly handsome caper spurge, upright as a little column. Factually an annual, it seeds itself so generously and has a habit of placing itself just where it knows it will look best, as though it were possessed of some natural architectural sense, that you need never bother about sowing it afresh.

I am very fond of *Euphorbia marginata*, unfortunately an annual, and unfortunately attractive to sparrows. They peck. I persist, however, for the sake of the green-and-silver effect of the striped leaves and the white bracts. If the caper spurge has an architectural quality, *Euphorbia marginata* has an heraldic quality: it might be dressed in a tabard. It is a native of the southern states of North America, where it is known as Snow-on-the-mountain.

I am very fond also of *Euphorbia pilosa*. This is a perennial, and grows in a neat little rounded clump of greenish-gold, about a foot high. It is at its best in spring, but very tidy all the year round. I had it once in association with the greenish viola *Irish Molly*, and a very happy association it was. Molly died on me, but the spurge heartlessly shows every sign of increasing in vigour.

The most exciting spurge I have got is called *Euphorbia griffithii*. It was collected in Tibet, and was given an Award of Merit a couple of years ago. It has the strangest combination of colouring: brown, orange and green, giving a general impression of rusty red, not unlike *Euphorbia sikkimensis*. Please, try this if you don't already know it. One root of it will rush all over the place within twelve months.

Then there is *Euphorbia Wulfenii*. I have never grown this, and I don't like to recommend plants without personal experience of them, but I realize that *E. Wulfenii* is a serious lapse on my part. It must be one of the most recommendable of the spurges.

June

Miniature gardens

The rheumatic, the sufferers from lumbago, and the merely elderly, would all be well advised to try a little experiment in sink or trough gardening. By sink or trough we mean either those old-fashioned stone sinks now rejected in favour of glazed porcelain or aluminium; or the stone drinking-troughs with which pigs and cattle were once content before they had heard of concrete. Repudiated now by man and beast, they can be picked up in a house-breaker's yard for a few shillings; and, raised to hand level on four little piers of brick or stone, may provide in this their second life a constant pleasure and interest to those keen gardeners who for one reason or another can no longer stoop or dig, but who still wish to fidget happily with their favourite occupation.

Fidget is perhaps the right word, for this is indeed a miniature form of gardening. The sink-gardener is like a jeweller working in precious stones. He makes his designs, trying experiments which he can alter when they fail to satisfy him, if he had the wisdom to keep a few pots in reserve. Out comes the offending colour, and in goes the befitting colour, neatly dropped in without any root disturbance.

Choose as deep a trough as possible, to get the maximum depth of soil. It must have a hole for drainage; and crocks spread over the whole bottom for the same purpose. The soil should be a mixture of fibrous loam, leaf-mould, sharp silver sand, and very finely broken-up bits of old flower-pots.

On top of this gritty bed you then arrange rocks or even flat stones. No one can dictate to you how to dispose your rocks, for this will be according to each person's fancy, but one can at least make some suggestions about what to plant. It is very important to keep everything to the right scale. Here is a short list of things which should do well: *Thymus serpyllum* for carpeting; *saxifrages* of the Kabschia or the encrusted kind; the tiny Alpine forget-me-not, *Myosotis rupicola*; the tiny Alpine poppy; *Bellis Dresden China*, a very bright pink little daisy; *Erinus alpinus*, pink; *Veronica Allionii*, violet spikes; *Allium cyaneum*, a five-inch-high blue garlic; and even the midget roses, *Rouletti* and *Oakington Ruby*; and the innumerable bulbs such as the early species crocuses (*Sieboldii*, *Tomasinianus*), and the early species tulips such as *linifolia*, bright red, or *dasystemon*, green and grey; or *Orphanidea*, bronze; and scillas and chionodoxas and grape hyacinths . . . leave readers to their imagination. There is plenty of scope.

A sense of colour

I have a gardening dodge which I find very useful. It concerns colour-schemes and plant-groupings. You know how quickly one forgets what one's garden has looked like during different weeks progressively throughout the year? One makes a mental note, or even a written note, and then the season changes and one forgets what one meant at the time. One has written 'Plant something yellow near the yellow tulips,' or 'Plant something tall behind the lupins,' and then autumn comes and plants have died down, and one scratches one's head trying to remember what on earth one meant by that.

My system is more practical. I observe, for instance, a

great pink, lacy crinoline of the May-flowering tamarisk, of which I put in two snippets years ago, and which now spreads the exuberance of its petticoats twenty feet wide over a neglected corner of the garden. What could I plant near it to enhance its colour? It must, of course, be something which will flower at the same time. So I try effects, picking flowers elsewhere, rather in the way that one makes a flower arrangement in the house, sticking them into the ground and then standing back to observe the harmony. The dusky, rosy *Iris Senlac* is just the right colour: I must split up my clumps as soon as they have finished flowering and make a group of those near the tamarisk for next May. The common pink columbine, almost a weed, would do well for underplanting, or some pink pansies, *Crimson Queen*, or the wine-red shades, as a carpet; and, for something really noble, the giant fox-tail lily, *Eremurus robustus*, eight to ten feet high. I cut, with reluctance, one precious spike from a distant group, and stick it in; it looks fine, like a cathedral spire flushed warm in the sunset. Undoubtedly I should have some *eremuri* next year with the plumy curtains of the tamarisk behind them, but the *eremuri* are too expensive and one cannot afford many of them.

This is just one example. One has the illusion of being an artist painting a picture – putting in a dash of colour here, taking out another dash of colour there, until the whole composition is to one's liking, and at least one knows exactly what effect will be produced twelve months hence.

A thyme lawn

Two years ago I had what I thought might be a bright idea. It has turned out so bright, in both senses of word, that I must pass it on.

92

I had two small windswept beds (the size was eight yards long by five yards wide each), divided by a path of paving stones down the middle. I tried every sort of thing in them, including a mad venture of hollyhocks, which, of course, got flattened by the prevailing south-west wind, however strongly we staked them. So then I decided I must have something very low growing, which would not suffer from the wind, and scrapped the hollyhocks, and dibbled in lots and lots of thyme, and now have a sort of lawn which, while it is densely flowering in purple and red, looks like a Persian carpet laid flat on the ground out of doors. The bees think that I have laid it for their special benefit. It really is a lovely sight; I do not want to boast, but I cannot help being pleased with it; it is so seldom that one's experiments in gardening are wholly successful.

The thyme we used was the cultivated or garden form of the wild thyme, *Thymus serpyllum*, in fact the form you see creeping about between paving-stones on paths and terraces. *Serpyllum* comes from the Latin *serpere*, to creep; think of serpent; and in fact two old English names for the wild thyme were serpille and serpolet. My serpolet lawn. . . . The Romans believed its fragrance to be a remedy for melancholia; and in later years, our own Elizabethan times, it was thought to cure sciatica and whooping cough, headache, frenzy, and lethargy.

We had the common purple sort, and the sort called *coccineus* to give the redder patches, and also a little of the white, which varied the pattern.

I have planted a few bulbs of small things in amongst the thyme, to give some interest in the spring, when the thyme is merely green. A patch of crocuses; a patch of the miniature narcissus; a patch of the little pink cyclamen. It occurs to me also that if you have not a flat bed to devote to a thyme-lawn you could fill a sunny bank with it. Steep grass banks are always awkward to mow, but the thyme would not need any mowing, and it should revel in a sunny exposure with the good drainage of a slope.

Alliums

Mr. William Robinson, in his classic work *The English Flower Garden*, was very scornful of the Alliums or ornamental garlics. He said that they were 'not of much value in the garden'; that they produced so many little bulblets as to make themselves too numerous; and that they smelt when crushed.

For once, I must disagree with that eminent authority. I think, on the contrary, that some of the Alliums have a high value in the June garden; far from objecting to a desirable plant making a spreading nuisance of itself, I am only too thankful that it should do so; and as for smelling nasty when crushed – well, who in his senses would wish wantonly to crush his own flowers?

Allium Rosenbachianum is extremely handsome, four feet tall, with big, rounded lilac heads delicately touched with green. Its leaves, however, are far from handsome, so it should be planted behind something which will conceal them. If you are by nature a hoarder, you can cut down the long stems after the flowers have faded and keep them with their seed-pods for what is known to florists as 'interior decoration' throughout the winter. Like most of the garlics, they demand a sunny, well-drained situation. They get better and better after the first year of planting.

Allium albo-pilosum, a Persian, my favourite, is lilac in colour, two feet high or so. *Allium cyaneum* is a mite, four inches only, blue, suitable for sinks or troughs, or any place where it can be observed at eye-level. The white-headed garlic, *Allium neapolitanum*, is useful for cutting; and is apparently indestructible.

Allium giganteum, five feet tall, is generally agreed to be the grandest of all. I bought a single one last year, and am now watching it anxiously. It should flower in July.

Honeysuckles

We all have associations with the familiar scents of our childhood, whether they be of sweet-briar on a moist evening, or of a red rose warmed by the sun, or of our native honeysuckle threading its way through a hedge. It is thus rather a shock to find some honeysuckles which have no scent at all, but which have flowers of such surprising beauty that they are worth growing for their colour alone.

Some of these are now flowering in my garden. I like and admire them, though I cannot love them in the way one loves the old sentimental kinds which always smelt so good. The ones with the huge yellow scentless flowers are called *Lonicera Tellmanniana* and *Lonicera tragophylla*. There is also a bright red-orange one, *Lonicera Brownii fuchsioides*. They seem to do well in sun or shade; trained against a wall, or scrambling over a fence. I never know whether I prefer them in sun or in shade. The sunshine paints a brilliance on them, with a varnishing brush of light; but in a shady corner they have the deep, secret glow of hidden things.

I have recently regretted that I did not plant more honeysuckles in my garden. I suppose that all gardeners are suddenly assailed by similar pangs of regret. Fortunately, in the case of the honeysuckles, which are fast-growing subjects, it is an omission which can be rectified this coming autumn.

For the scented ones, I shall plant the Early Dutch, flowering in May and June: and the late Dutch, flowering from July to September or October. These are both related to our native honeysuckle. For winter flowering, I have already got *Lonicera fragrantissima* and its perhaps better fellow, *Lonicera Standishii*. They do not flower very exuberantly, in my experience, but even a couple of sprays picked in January are welcome and will scent a whole room.

Ixias

Brave gardeners who have a sunny corner to spare, at the foot of a south wall for choice, and a poor sandy soil, should plant some bulbs of Ixia, the South African Corn-lily. It is a graceful thing, about eighteen inches high, with rush-like leaves and a flower-spike in various colours: white, yellow, coral-pink, and sometimes striped like the boiled sweets of our childhood. There is also a particularly lovely and rather strange variety, green with a black centre, *Ixia viridiflora*, which is more expensive.

Ixias are not entirely hardy, though hardier than the freesias which they somewhat resemble. Very sharp drainage, deep planting of about six inches, and a little cover throughout our damp winter, should, however, ensure their survival, and those which fail to reappear can be replaced annually for half a crown. Of course, the more you can plant, the better. They flower in June and take up very little room. They are ideal for picking, as they last a long time in water and arrange themselves with thin and slender elegance in a tall glass.

They do also very well as pot-plants in a cold greenhouse or a conservatory, not requiring any heat but only protection from frost. If you grow them this way, you must disregard the advice to plant them six inches deep, and cover them with only an inch or so of soil – sandy loam and a handful of leaf-mould mixed to each pot, and crocks for drainage at the bottom.

I do hope you will order some Ixias for planting next October or November. I admit that they are apt to die out after a year or so; but to those gardeners who have a poor, starved soil and a warm corner they are a God-given present in June.

Peonies

Often one is asked for plants which will flourish in semi-shade, and in the month of June the noble peony comes to mind. (I mean the herbaceous sort, not the species or the Tree-peony.) It always seems to me that the herbaceous peony is the very epitome of June. Larger than any rose, it has something of the cabbage rose's voluminous quality; and when it finally drops from the vase, it sheds its vast petti-coats with a bump on the table, all in an intact heap, much as a rose will suddenly fall, making us look up from our book or conversation, to notice for one moment the death of what had still appeared to be a living beauty.

To be practical, there is much to recommend the peony. I will make a list of its virtues. It is a very long-lived plant, increasing yearly in vigour if you will only leave it undis-turbed. It likes to stay put. It will, as I said, flourish in half-shade, and indeed its brag of size and colour gains from the broken light of overhanging branches. It doesn't object to an alkaline soil, a great advantage to those who cannot grow lime-hating plants in their garden. Rabbits do not appear to care for its young shoots. Slugs don't care for it either; and the only disease it may seriously suffer from is *wilt*, a fungus,

Botrytis. If this appears, you must cut out the diseased bits and burn them; but in the many years I have grown peonies in my garden I have, touch wood, never found any trace of disease amongst my gross Edwardian swagger ladies.

The secret of growing the herbaceous peonies is to plant them very shallow and give them a deep, rich root-run of manure for their roots to find as they go down in search of nourishment. Then they will go ahead, and probably out-live the person who planted them, so that his or her grand-child will be picking finer flowers fifty years hence.

Some flowering shrubs

There are two very pretty May-June flowering shrubs not difficult to grow but for some reason not very commonly seen. They go well together, both being of the same shade of a delicate shell-pink and both belonging to the same botanical family (*Caprifoliaceae*), which includes the more familiar Weigelas and the honeysuckles, with small trumpet-shaped flowers dangling from graceful sprays. These two shrubs are *Kolkwitzia amabilis* and *Dipelta floribunda*.

Kolkwitzia comes into flower a little later than *Dipelta*, and thus provides a useful succession in the same colouring; in other words, a combination of the two would ensure a cloud of pale pink over a considerable number of weeks. It ought to be planted in front of the *Dipelta*, as it tends to make a more rounded bush, whereas the *Dipelta* grows taller and looser, and flops enough to require a few tall stakes. Both come from China, and each deserves the other's adjective, as well as their own, for they are both amiable and floriferous.

While on the subject of May flowering shrubs, I might mention *Rubus deliciosus*. This comes from the Rocky

Mountains, and is a bramble, but not thorny. I cannot imagine why this lovely and easy-going thing should be so foolishly neglected. If you are acquainted with the big, single white rose *Nevada*, you will readily make a mental picture of *Rubus deliciosus*, for I notice that people usually mistake it for the rose until, on looking closer, they become surprised to find it blowing among leaves like the leaves of a blackcurrant. It will reach 8 ft. and more in height, great arching sprays which may require a few bamboo canes for a light support. Apart from this it involves no labour, except an occasional cutting-out of dead wood.

This is a *rubus* for May, but it has a Himalayan relation in *Rubus biflorus*, the white-washed bramble, which is grown less for the sake of its insignificant flowers than for the beauty of its pure white stems in winter. Tall ghosts, they make a surprising apparition in the winter landscape, suggesting a plant permanently coated with rime. It likes a rich soil, and you have to cut down the stems which have flowered, and probably fruited, the previous year because the young growth is what you need to encourage and retain.

Old roses

These June evenings, when for once in a way we are allowed a deep warm sloping sunlight, how rare and how precious they are. They ought to be accompanied by fireflies, wild gold flakes in the air, but in this island we have to make do with tethered flowers instead. Amongst these, the huge lax bushes of the old roses must take an honoured place.

The old roses have recently wriggled their way back into favour, and small wonder. They give so little trouble for so great a reward. By the old roses I mean the Cabbage, the Moss, the Centifolias, the Gallicas, the Musks and the

Damasks whose very names suggest a honeyed southern dusk.

I know that they have neither the neatness nor the brilliance of the Hybrid Teas, and I know also that most of them suffer from the serious drawback of flowering only once during a season, but what incomparable lavishness they give, while they are about it. There is nothing scrimpy or stingy about them. They have a generosity which is as desirable in plants as in people.

In this revival of the old roses, we surely have rediscovered a form of gardening enjoyed by our Victorian grandparents. I hold in my mind the vision of a rose-garden planted in 1870, crammed with old roses that had run about all over the place on their own roots, going into an untidy wilderness, a tangle of roses I could not name. I took a great rosarian with me, and shall never forget her excitement, dashing about, saying that she could not name them either, but must take cuttings in order to preserve these old treasures from loss and destruction.

Fortunately, it is now possible to buy the old roses from some nurserymen who specialize in them. Their catalogues read like one long poem of names: Reine des Violettes, Cardinal Richelieu, Nuits d'Young, Tuscany, Rosa Mundi, the striped pink-and-white rose, which many people confuse with the York and Lancaster. There are so many of them that it is not possible for me to give more than a brief suggestion about what to plant if you have the space to afford in your garden.

Iris sibirica

I would like to render thanks to the *Iris sibirica*, which arises from reedy stems in delicate flower-heads of dark purple, lavender, and white. It varies in its colour, and that is one of its most attractive characteristics. If you hold it up against the light, you will perceive its delicate veining.

It is the easiest of things to grow, for it will do well by the waterside in a fairly damp bed, although it does not like being drowned under water all the year round. It will do equally well in an ordinary bed or border, in fact, it will do its best for us anywhere, even to the extent of seeding itself and appearing in unexpected places, as I have recently noticed in my own garden.

I say 'recently', because I was astonished to find *Iris sibirica* flowering in corners where I knew I had never deliberately planted it, and could not imagine how it had come there, until I discovered that the seedlings of this iris take no longer than two years to reach their flowering stage. The seedlings would not necessarily come true to the colour of their parents, but one might always have the luck to raise a particularly good form. For this reason it would be worth while growing a drill of home-saved seed in an unwanted strip of ground and seeing what would result after two years' waiting.

The same may be said of that exquisite relation of *Iris sibirica*, the almost black little iris called *chrysographes*. It also will flower from seed within two years. It comes from China and is perhaps a plant for the connoisseur rather than for the amateur gardener who just wants the mass effect he will gain more readily from the tall and slender *sibirica*. *Iris chrysographes* grows only a foot high and needs looking close into for a full perception of its beauty. Yet it is quite easy to grow, given a place that never dries out and is rich in humus.

Still, *Iris sibirica* is for everyone, forming large clumps of perhaps rather untidy leaves, whose untidiness is redeemed by the wealth of tall flowers rising in June and persisting for several weeks as the quantity of buds succeed one another in their opening.

More roses

Drunk on roses, I look round and wonder which to recommend. Among the climbers, I do not believe that I have ever mentioned *Lawrence Johnston*, a splendid yellow, better than the very best butter, and so vigorous as to cover 12 ft. of wall within two seasons. It does not seem to be nearly so well known as it ought to be, even under its old name *Hidcote Yellow*, although it dates back to 1923 and received an Award of Merit from the R.H.S. in 1948. The bud, of a beautifully pointed shape, opens into a loose, nearly-single flower which does not lose its colour up to the very moment when it drops. Eventually it will attain a height of 30 ft., but if you cannot afford the space for so rampant a grower, you have a sister seedling in *Le Rêve*, indistinguishable as to flower and leaf, but more restrained as to growth.

There is a fairly new hybrid musk, *Grandmaster*, which would associate well as a bush planted in front of either *Lawrence Johnston* or *Le Rêve*. This is an exquisite thing, a great improvement on the other hybrid musk, *Buff Beauty*, though that in all conscience is lovely enough. *Grandmaster* is nearly single, salmon-coloured on the outside and a very pale gold within, scentless, alas, which one does not expect of a musk, but that fault must be overlooked for the extreme beauty of the bush spattered all over as it were with large golden butterflies. These shrubby roses are invaluable, giving so little trouble and filling so wide an area at so little cost.

If the yellows are not to your liking, you have a perfect

rose-pink in *Gallica complicata*. Enormous single flowers borne all the length of the very long sprays. I cannot think why it should be called *complicata*, for it has a simplicity and purity of line which might come straight out of a Chinese drawing. This is a real treasure, if you can give it room to toss itself about as it likes; and whether you lightly stake it upright or allow it to trail must depend upon how you feel about it. Personally I think that its graceful untidiness is part of its charm, but whatever you do with it you can depend upon it to fill any corner with its renewed surprise in June.

Growing flowers up trees

So often there is a valueless old tree in a garden, it might be an apple or one of those old pears whose fruits never get any softer than pebbles, or even a dead tree fit only for the woodman's axe.

> Woodman, spare that tree!
> Touch not a single bough,

as George Pope Morris appealingly wrote some time in the last century, going on to say that in youth it had sheltered him and therefore deserved his protection. Today, following the example of William Robinson in his once famous garden at Gravetye, he would doubtless have used it as a prop for some wreathing, writhing climber, as Mr. Robinson tossed roses, honeysuckles, clematis and vines in profusion and let them find their way upwards towards the light. Swarthy sombre trees, say a Lawson's cypress or a thuya, are especially suitable for such treatment, since the dark background enhances the beauty of the climber's flower and also gives thick and twiggy support. The familiar *macrocarpa* of hedges will grow to a tree of pyramidal shape and considerable height and, with its lower branches trimmed away, exposing the trunk, is perhaps the best substitute at our command for the Italian cypress. A vigorous climber, such as *Clematis montana*, should soon clothe it to the top; this small-flowered clematis can be had in its white form, or in the pink variety, *rubra*. The so-called Russian vine, *Polygonum baldschuanicum*, most rapid of climbers, will go to a height of 20 ft. or more, and is attractive with its feathery plumes of a creamy white. It should scarcely be necessary to emphasize the value of the wistarias for similar purpose.

One advantage of this use of climbers for a small garden is the saving of ground space. The soil, however, should be richly made up in the first instance, as the tree-roots will rob it grossly, and will also absorb most of the moisture, so see to it that a newly planted climber does not lack water during its first season, before it has had time to become established and is sending out its own roots far enough or deep enough to get beyond the worst of the parched area.

Nursery flowers

There is something in all of us which responds to something we have known in our childhood. It may be a scent, or a touch, or a sight, or anything which evokes a memory. For some of us this evocation arises from the recollection of flowers we saw growing in our grandparents' gardens and now search for in vain.

Why should they have gone out of fashion, the dear old tenants of the kitchen garden border? They were not very grand, so they were usually relegated to the strip between the espalier apples and the path. They shared that strip with the old double primroses, and the Hen-and-Chicken daisy, and some Dusty Miller auriculas, all living very happily together. The plants I am thinking of now, came behind these lowly growers, into the middle-height of the border.

They all had English names by which we knew them. There was the Bleeding Heart or Lyre Flower, more familiar under that name than as *Dicentra* or *Dielytra spectabilis*. One could pull each locket of the Bleeding Heart into different shapes, the most pleasing turning into a little pink-and-white ballet dancer. If you don't believe me, try it. Then there was the Masterwort, or *Astrantia*, a greenish-white or pale pink, a reliable old plant for the border, so seldom seen now. Then there was Solomon's Seal, *Polygonatum multiflorum*; and *Smilacina racemosa*, both plants for a shady place, with grand green leaves and long strands of white moonlight flowers. The Smilacina has the advantage of a strong scent and of lasting very well in water. It deserves to be grown much more extensively.

Another old plant I like very much is *Tradescantia virginiana*, the Spiderwort named after John Tradescant, gardener to Charles I and Henrietta Maria. It is also called the Trinity Flower, owing to its three petals of a rich violet, curiously lurking amongst the grassy leaves. Perfectly hardy, it has a very long flowering season from June onwards into the autumn. It likes the sun, but will also put up with some shade. Do not confuse it with another Tradescantia, which is a trailing plant for the greenhouse, with green-and-white striped leaves.

Columbines

Not nearly enough use is made of that airy flower, the modern columbine. Even our old native *Aquilegia vulgaris* has its charm. Who could resist anything nicknamed

Granny's Bonnet or Doves-round-a-dish? I never have the heart to tear it out from wherever it has chosen to sow itself, though I know that it is little more than a weed and is a nuisance in that it hybridizes to the detriment of the choicer kinds. In fact, there are few flowers better disposed to hybridize amongst themselves, or, as one nurseryman puts it, 'their morals leave much to be desired.' In the case of the columbines, however, this is part of their attraction, for it means you may get chance seedlings of a colour you never anticipated.

Let me list their other advantages. They are perennial, which saves a lot of bother. They are hardy. They are light and graceful in a mixed bunch. They will put up with a certain amount of shade. They are easily grown from seed, and may be had in a surprising range of height and hue, from the tiny blue *alpina* whose inch of stature makes it suitable for rockeries, to the 3-ft. long-spurred hybrids in yellow, white, blue, mauve, pink, crimson-and-gold; and even, if you want something really out of the way, in green-and-brown. This last one is called *viridiflora*, and is about a foot high.

For any lucky person with the space to spare, I could imagine a small enclosed garden or, say, a three-sided court-yard such as you often find in old farmhouses. If the court-yard happens to be paved with flagstones, so much the better, for, as I never tire of saying, plants love to get between the cracks and send their roots down into the cool reaches of the soil beneath, thus preserving themselves from the minor enemy of frost and from the major enemy of damp. It is just such a little walled garden or courtyard that I envisage, glowing with a coloration of columbines.

July

Raising your own plants

This is a good moment to think of your future stock. Plants, and even seeds, are expensive to buy, but by raising your own nursery you can get plants by the thousand if you wish, for no cost beyond your own time and labour. It is well worth saving the seeds of annuals, biennials, and even perennials, either from your own garden or the gardens of friends who may have better varieties than you have. They must be quite ripe, and can be stored in little air-tight tins, such as the tins that typewriter ribbons come in, and sown in September when they will have time to make sturdy growth before the winter. Pansies, Indian pinks, columbines, foxgloves, forget-me-not, primrose, polyanthus, anemones, lupins, and many other garden flowers can be thus harvested. Sow them thinly in drills on a finely pulverized seed-bed, and move them to their flowering quarters in the spring.

Remember that home-saved seeds will not necessarily come true, as the insects will have interfered with them. All the same, it is worth trying, and you might even get an interesting hybrid.

Lilies may also be raised from seed, instead of paying half a crown or more for a single bulb. *Lilium regale* will come up as thick as mustard and cress by this method; you will have to wait two or possibly three years before the bulbs come to flowering size, but think of the economy and of the staggered crop that you can raise, if you sow even one little row of seed every year.

Clematis will grow from seed, and so will broom; but as both these hate being disturbed it is advisable to grow them single in small pots, when they can be tipped out without noticing that anything has happened.

Cutting of many flowering shrubs such as ceanothus, can be taken in July. Set them very firmly in a drill filled with sharp sand, in the open in the shade. As with rose cuttings, you should put in more than you need. A closed frame or even a hand-light put over cuttings for the first ten days or so will help them to strike, but they will give quite good results without this. Remember the hormone preparations recommended for rose cuttings will very greatly help any cutting to strike: simple instructions are supplied with the bottle.

Alstroemerias

There are some moments when I feel pleased with my garden, and other moments when I despair. The pleased moments usually happen in spring, and last up to the middle of June. By that time all the freshness has gone off; everything has become heavy; everything has lost that adolescent look, that look of astonishment at its own youth. The middle-age spread has begun.

It is then that the *Alstroemerias* come into their own. Lumps of colour. . . . They are in flower now, so this is the opportunity to go and see them, either in a local nurseryman's plot, or in a private garden, or at a flower show. The yellow Peruvian lily, *A. aurantiaca*, was and is a common sight in cottage gardens and old herbaceous borders, where it was regarded almost as a weed, but it has been superseded by the far more beautiful *Ligtu* hybrids, in varied colours of coral and buff, and by *A. haemantha*, a brilliant orange. (Keep the orange away from the coral, for they dot mix well together, and whoever it was who said Nature made no mistakes in colour-harmony was either colour-blind or a sentimentalist. Nature sometimes makes the most hideous mistakes; and it is up to us gardeners to control and correct them.)

The *Ligtu* hybrids of *Alstroemeria*, and also the orange *A. haemantha*, can and should be grown from seed. You sow the seed in February or March, where you intend the plant to grow and flower. I am sure I am right in recommending this method. One reason is that the seed germinates very freely; another reason is that the roots of *Alstroemeria* are extremely brittle, and thus are difficult to transplant; and the third reason is that plants are expensive to buy and may fail owing to the difficulty of transplantation. Therefore I say sow your own seed and wait for two years before your clumps come to their fulfilment.

They demand full sun and good drainage, by which I mean that they would not like any shade or a water-logged soil. They are sun-lovers. They also demand staking, not stiff staking, but a support of twiggy branches to hold them up; otherwise they flop and snap and lose their beauty, lying flat after a thunderstorm of rain or a sudden gale, such as we get from time to time in our usually temperate country. This is a counsel of caution. Prop up your *Alstroemerias*, if you take my advice to grow them, by twiggy pea-sticks.

They are the perfect flower for cutting, lasting weeks in water in the house.

The seedlings would like a little protection in winter if there is a hard frost. Some bracken will do, scattered over them. Once established, they are hardy enough to withstand anything but a particularly bad winter. It is only the young that are tender, needing a little love and care.

More about magnolias

The flowers of *Magnolia grandiflora* look like great white pigeons settling among dark leaves. This is an excellent plant for covering an ugly wall-space, being evergreen and fairly rapid of growth. It is not always easy to know what to put against a new red-brick wall; pinks and reds are apt to swear, and to intensify the already-too-hot colour; but the cool green of the magnolia's glossy leaves and the utter purity of its bloom make it a safe thing to put against any background, however trying. Besides, the flower in itself is of such splendid beauty. I have just been looking into the heart of one. The texture of the petals is of a dense cream; they should not be called white; they are ivory, if you can imagine ivory and cream stirred into a thick paste, with all the softness and smoothness of youthful human flesh; and the scent, reminiscent of lemon, was overpowering.

There is a theory that magnolias do best under the protection of a north or west wall, and this is true of the spring-flowering kinds, which are only too liable to damage from morning sunshine after a frosty night, when you may come out after breakfast to find nothing but a lamentable tatter of brown suède; but *grandiflora*, flowering in July and August, needs no such consideration. In fact, it seems to do better on a sunny exposure, judging by the two plants I have in my garden. I tried an experiment, as usual. One of them is against a shady west wall, and never carries more than half a dozen buds; the other, on a glaring south-east wall, normally carries twenty to thirty. The reason, clearly, is that the summer sun is necessary to ripen the wood on which the flowers will be borne. What they don't like is drought when they are young i.e. before their roots have had time to go far in search of moisture; but as they will quickly indicate their disapproval by beginning to drop their yellowing leaves, you can be on your guard with a can of water, or several cans, from the rain-water butt.

Goliath is the best variety. Wires should be stretched along the wall on vine-eyes for convenience of future tying. This will save a lot of trouble in the long run, for the magnolia should eventually fill a space at least twenty feet wide by twenty feet high or more, reaching right up to the eaves of the house. The time may come when you reach out of your bedroom window to pick a ghostly flower in the summer moonlight, and then you will be sorry if you find it has broken away from the wall and is fluttering on a loose branch, a half-captive pigeon trying desperately to escape.

Some favourite roses

I am astonished, and even alarmed, by the growth which certain roses will make in the course of a few years. There is one called *Madame Plantier*, which we planted at the foot of a worthless old apple tree, vaguely hoping that it might cover a few feet of the trunk. Now it is 15 feet high with a girth of 15 yards, tapering towards the top like the waist of a Victorian beauty and pouring down in a vast crinoline stitched all over with its white sweet-scented clusters of flower.

Madame Plantier dates back, in fact to 1835, just two years before Queen Victoria came to the throne, so she and the Queen may be said to have grown up together towards the crinolines of their maturity. Queen Victoria is dead, but

Madame Plantier still very much alive. I go out to look at her in the moonlight: she gleams, a pear-shaped ghost, contriving to look both matronly and virginal. She has to be tied up round her tree, in long strands, otherwise she would make only a big straggly bush; we have found that the best method is to fix a sort of tripod of bean-poles against the tree and tie the strands to that.

Another favourite white rose of mine is *Paul's Lemon Pillar*. It should not be called white. A painter might see it as greenish, suffused with sulphur-yellow, and its great merit lies not only in the vigour of its growth and wealth of flowering, but also in the perfection of its form. The shapeliness of each bud has a sculptural quality which suggests curled shavings of marble, if one may imagine marble made of the softest ivory suède. The full-grown flower is scarcely less beautiful; and when the first explosion of bloom is over, a carpet of thick white petals covers the ground, so dense as to look as though it had been deliberately laid.

The old *Madame Alfred Carrière* is likewise in full flower. Smaller than Paul's rose, and with no pretension to a marmoreal shape. *Madame Alfred*, white, flushed with shell-pink, has the advantage of a sweet, true-rose scent, and will grow to the eaves of any reasonably proportioned house, even on a west or north wall. I should like to see every Airey house in this country rendered invisible behind this curtain of white and green.

Eremuri

Visitors to June and July flower-shows may have been surprised, pleased, and puzzled by enormous spikes, six to eight feet in height, which looked something like a giant lupin, but which, on closer inspection, proved to be very different. They were to be seen in various colours: pale yellow, buttercup-yellow, greenish-yellow, white and greenish-white, pink, and a curious fawn-pink which is as hard to describe, because as subtle, as the colour of a chaffinch's breast.

These were *Eremuri*, sometimes called the fox-tail lily, and sometimes the giant asphodel. They belong, in fact, to the botanical family of the lilies, but, unlike most lilies, they do not grow from a bulb. They grow from a starfish-like root, which is brittle and needs very careful handling when you transplant it. I think this is probably the reason why some people fail to establish the eremurus satisfactorily. It should be moved in the last weeks of September or the first weeks of October, and it should be moved with the least possible delay. The roots should never be allowed to wait, shrivelling, out of the ground. Plant them instantly, as soon as they arrive from the nursery. Spread out the roots, flat, in a rather rich loamy soil, and cover them over with some bracken to protect them from frost during their first winter. Plant them under the shelter of a hedge, if you can; they dislike a strong wind, and the magnificence of their spires will show up better for the backing of a dark hedge. They like lime and sunshine.

Thus established, the fox-tail lily should give increasing delight as the years go by. They get better and better as they grow older and older, throwing up more and more spires of flower from each crown of their star-fish root. There are several sorts obtainable; the giant *Eremurus robustus*, which flowers in June, and then the smaller ones, the Shelford hybrids and the Warei hybrids in their strange colours. Splendid things; torches of pale colour, towering, dwarfing the ordinary little annuals. Aristocrats of the garden.

Daphnes

The bushes of Mesereon or *Daphne Mezereum* should now be hung with their fruits, if the birds have not already pecked them off. It is well worth while to save and sow some of them, for they germinate very freely and a crop of young plants is the result. I am told on good authority that the Daphne is not very long-lived but has a better expectation of life when it is growing on its own roots, i.e. has not been grafted, so the moral of growing it from seed (or cuttings) is obvious.

The Mesereon seems to share with the Madonna lily a predilection for cottage gardens. Bushes five feet high and four feet wide carry their wine-coloured bloom on the naked stems year after year in February and March in a luxuriance unknown to grander gardens where far more trouble is taken about them. Cottagers apparently just stick it in everywhere, when, with the perversity of an inverted snobbishness, it grows. It is useless to try to explain this peculiar psychology of certain plants. One must accept it and do the best one can to reproduce the conditions they appear to enjoy.

After struggling for years to induce *Daphne Mezereum* to thrive in my garden, I have at last achieved a miserable degree of success by planting it in a mixture of leaf-mould and sand, in the broken shade of some trees of Kentish cobnuts. This is the treatment I would recommend: a spongy soil with overhead shade in summer. After all, the Mesereon is sometimes claimed as a native of Britain, growing in woods, so it seems reasonable to plant it in the sort of soil it would be likely to encounter in its natural habitat, full of decayed leaves and humus, rich with the fallen wealth of centuries.

On the other hand, some people will tell you that it never thrives better than in a hot, dry place, such as a gravelly path right up against the house. So what is one to believe?

There are two kinds of *Daphne Mezereum*. One is the familiar claret-coloured one, pink as a *vin Rosé* held up to the light in a *carafe*. The other is white, *Daphne Mezereum alba*. They have different coloured berries. The familiar one has bright red berries. The white form has bright yellow berries. I would strongly advise you to poke some seeds of both into small pots, instead of letting the birds have them. Daphnes do not transplant well, and should always be tipped straight out of a pot, like a broom or a clematis.

I have not observed seed on any of the other Daphnes, with the exception of the scentless *D. acutiloba*, but there is a prostrate one called *Blagayana*, ivory in colour and intensely sweet-scented in the early spring. This likes to be layered and weighted down with stones at every point where the layer has been inserted. It will then spread outwards into a mat of fresh growth, which may eventually attain a width of six feet or more. It is a delight to pick in the cold days of March, to bring into the warmth of a room when the honeyed smell floats round into stray corners with a suggestion of bees and summer airs. The same is true of *Daphne odora*, but that unfortunately is not quite as hardy and needs the protection of glass throughout the frosty months, either in a greenhouse or under a cloche.

The importance of scale

I believe that one ought always to regard a garden in terms of architecture as well as of colour. One has huge lumps of, let us say, the shrub roses making large voluminous bushes

115

like a Victorian crinoline, or flinging themselves about in wild sprays; or, putting it another way, some plants make round fat bushes, and seem to demand a contrast in a tall sharp plant, say delphiniums, stiking up in a cathedral spire of bright blue amongst the roses instead of in the orthodox way at the back of a herbaceous border. It is all a question of shape. Architectural shape, demanding the pointed thin ones amongst the fat rounds, as a minaret rises above the dome of a mosque.

Let me say here, for the small garden, that one might happily cause some spikes of the pink *Linaria Canon J. Went* to rise above a carpeting of low pansies or violas. This Linaria comes true from seed; sows itself everywhere like a welcome, not an unwelcome, weed; and is as pretty a thing as you could wish to have in quantities for picking for the house indoors.

Another fine thing to make great steeples is *Yucca gloriosa*. This will tower in a vast heavy ivory pyramid in July, of a powerful architectural value. It does not flower every year, so you must have at least three plants in order to get a yearly blooming, and for this you need a certain amount of space; but if the smaller garden can spare even three yards, *Yucca gloriosa* will come as a fine surprise on the grand scale in July, and will carry out my contention that you want variety of shape and height to make an aesthetic composition instead of just an amorphous muddle. The Yucca, being a child of the desert in Mexico and some of the hotter parts of the United States, such as California, likes the driest possible place and the sunniest, but on the whole accommodates itself very obligingly to our soil and climate.

Ruthlessness in gardening

By this time of the year, most of our plants have grown into their full summer masses, and this is the moment when the discerning gardener goes round not only with his notebook but also with his secateurs and with that invaluable instrument on a pole 8 ft. long, terminated by a parrot's beak, which will hook down and sever any unwanted twig as easily as crooking your finger.

A bit of judicious cutting, snipping and chopping here and there will often make the whole difference. It may expose an aspect never noticed before, because overhanging branches had obscured it. It may reveal a coloured clump in the distance, hitherto hidden behind some overgrown bush of thorn or other unwanted rubbish. It is like being a landscape gardener on a small scale – and what gardener can afford to garden on the grand scale nowadays? It must also be like being a painter, giving the final touches to his canvas: putting just a dash of blue or yellow or red where it is wanted to complete the picture and to make it come together in a satisfactory whole.

This is the chance and the opportunity for the good gardener to go round his garden and make his notes for his future planting. He will observe gaps, and will ask himself how he is to fill those gaps up by new plants in the autumn. He will look through catalogues and will order plants recklessly.

Gardening is largely a question of mixing one sort of plant with another sort of plant, and of seeing how they marry happily together; and if you see that they don't marry happily, then you must hoick one of them out and be quite ruthless about it. That is the only way to garden. The true gardener must be brutal, and imaginative for the future.

The white garden at Sissinghurst

Provided one does not run the idea to death, and provided one has enough room, it is interesting to make a one-colour garden. It is something more than merely interesting. It is great fun and endlessly amusing as an experiment, capable of perennial improvement, as you take away the things that don't fit in, or that don't satisfy you, and replace them by something you like better.

There are two small internal gardens of this sort within my own garden. One of them is a typical cottage garden, a muddle of flowers, but all of them in the range of colour you might find in a sunset. I used to call it the sunset garden in my own mind before I even started to plant it up. I will not write about this now, for the sunset colours seem too hot in this month of July. I will write, rather, about the grey, green, white, silver garden which looks so cool on a summer evening.

I should like to use the old word *garth* for it, meaning a small piece of enclosed ground, usually beside a house or other building, for it is entirely enclosed, on one side by a high yew hedge and on the other sides by pink brick walls and a little Tudor house. It is divided into square beds by paths edged with lavender and box. But, as it is difficult to convey any impression of a place without the help of photographs, it would be wiser to confine myself to a list of the plants used to produce the cool, almost glaucous, effect we have aimed at.

There is an under-planting of various artemisias, including the old aromatic Southernwood; the silvery *Cineraria maritima*; the grey santolina or Cotton Lavender; and the creeping *Achillea ageratifolia*. Dozens of the white Regale lily (grown from seed) come up through these. There are white delphiniums of the Pacific strain; white eremurus, white foxgloves in a shady place on the north side of a wall; the foam of gypsophila; the white shrubby *Hydrangea grandiflora*; white cistus; white Tree peonies; *Buddleia nivea*; white campanulas and the white form of *Platycodon Mariesii*, the Chinese bell-flower. There is a group of the giant Arabian thistle, pure silver, 8 ft. high. Two little Sea Buckthorns, and the grey willow-leaved *Pyrus salicifolia* sheltering the grey leaden statue of a Vestal Virgin. Down the central path goes an avenue of white climbing roses, straggling up old almond trees. Later on there will be white Japanese anemones and some white dahlias; but I do not like to think of later on. It is bad enough to have turned over into July, with the freshness of another May and June gone for ever.

The acanthus

The expression *foliage plants* carries something of a Victorian sound for us, like the echoing of a gong through a linoleumed, encrusted boarding-house, but in spite of this grim association some of the foliage plants hold a high decorative value in the garden. They fill up gaps in the border, and richly deserve to be called handsome.

I am thinking in particular of the acanthus. This is a plant with a classical tradition, for it provided Greek architects with the design for the Corinthian capital to their columns. The form of acanthus they used must have been *Acanthus spinosus*, or *spinosissimus*, which has dark green leaves and a most prickly spike of pale purple bracts, at least 18 in. in length, very showy in July. For some odd reason it is popularly known as Bear's Breeches, though I should be sorry for any bear that had to wear them.

The form called *Acanthus mollis*, or *mollis latifolius*, has soft, rounded leaves of a paler green. It is less vicious than the spiny one, but on the whole I like the spiny one better.

Natives of the Mediterranean region, they naturally prefer a sunny place, but they will put up with a certain amount of shade. One is always grateful to plants that will consent to grow in that awkward corner where the sun penetrates only for a few hours during the day. Another obliging characteristic of the acanthus is that it will do very well as a plant in tubs or big pots, which you can stand about at your pleasure wherever you need them, on paths, or on steps, or on a terrace, or on any angle that the design of your garden suggests.

If you don't take kindly to my recommendation of the acanthus will you consider the *Funkia* or *Hosta*, the Plantain Lily? This is another foliage-plant, with large grey-green leaves and a spike of green-white flowers in July. It prefers a damp situation, but will grow anywhere you ask it to. It took me years of gardening to appreciate the pale beauty of its leaves and flowers, but now that I have learnt to look at them in the right way, I can begin to see what other gardeners meant when they extolled the merits of the *Funkia*.

One has a lot, an endless lot, to learn when one sets out to be a gardener.

Dead-heading

Dead-heading the roses on a summer evening is an occupation to carry us back into a calmer age and a different century. Queen Victoria might still be on the throne. All is quiet in the garden; the paths are pale; our silent satellite steals up the sky; even the aeroplanes have gone to roost and our own nerves have ceased to twangle. There is no sound except the hoot of an owl, and the rhythmic snip-snip of our own secateurs, cutting the dead heads off, back to a new bud, to provoke new growth for the immediate future.

A pleasurable occupation for us, when we have the time to spare, it must be even more pleasurable to the roses. They get relieved of those heavy rain-sodden lumps of spent flowers which are no good to themselves or to anyone else. There is something satisfying in the thought that we are doing good both to our rose-bushes and to ourselves in our snip-snip back towards the young shoot longing to develop, and something most gratifying in watching the pale green shoot lengthening inch by inch in a surprisingly short time.

The shrubby roses have lasted longer than usual this year, presumably because no hot days have burnt them up, but they are rapidly going over and their short season is a thing of the past. I notice that the *Rosa alba* known as Great Maiden's Blush holds her flowers longer than most. This is a very beautiful old rose, many-petalled, of an exquisite shell-pink clustering among the grey-green foliage, extremely sweet-scented, and for every reason perfect for filling a squat bowl indoors. In the garden she is not squat at all, growing 6 to 7 ft. high and wide in proportion, thus demanding a good deal of room, perhaps too much in a small border but lovely and reliable to fill a stray corner.

All the old roses have a touch of romance about them; the Great Maiden's Blush has more than a touch of romance in her various names alone. She has also been called *La Séduisante*, and *Cuisse de Nymphe* or the Nymph's Thigh. When she blushed a particularly deep pink, she was called *Cuisse de Nymphe Emue*. I will not insult the French language by attempting to translate this highly expressive name. I would suggest only that Cyrano de Bergerac would have appreciated the implication, and that any young couple with an immature garden and an even more immature pram-age daughter might well plant the Great Maiden alias *La Séduisante*.

The bell-flower

An effective splash of truly imperial purple may be had in the July-August border with a group of the Chinese bell-flower, *Platycodon grandiflorum*. It may be raised from seed sown in spring, though, being an herbaceous perennial, it cannot be expected to flower during the first summer of its life. True, there is a variety called *praecox*, for which a first-season flowering is claimed, but I cannot speak of it from experience.

The bell-flower or balloon-flower as it is sometimes called, resembles a campanula of a singularly rich colour, and does, in fact, belong to the same botanical family. Its shape charms me, when it first appears as a five-sided bud like a tiny lantern, as tightly closed as though its little seams had been stitched together, with the further charm that you can pop it like a fuchsia, if you are so childishly minded. This, I need hardly say, is not good for the eventual flower. Left to its natural development, it expands into a five-petalled bell of deep violet, so beautifully veined that it is worth holding a single bloom up to the light, for it is one of those blooms which repay a close examination, revealing not only the delicate veining but also the pale stamens grouped round the sapphire-blue of the pistil. Such examination may be a private pleasure, and is unlikely to be the principal reason for which we grow this sumptuous alien from China and Manchuria. It is for the splash in the border that it will be chiefly esteemed, a value scarcely to be exaggerated. I should like to see it associated with the feathery spires of *Thalictrum dipterocarpum*, a Meadow Rue, especially the variety called

Hewitt's Double, the Maidenhair-fern-like foliage and the cloud of innumerable small mauve flowers of the thalictrum coming up through the greater solidity of the purple bell-flower; but alas, the thalictrum will have nothing to say to me, patiently though I may plant and replant it, so I must content myself with recommending the idea to other, more fortunate, people.

The bell-flower, at any rate, presents no difficulty and seems completely happy in ordinary soil in the sun, near the front of the border, for it grows no taller than 18 in. to 2 ft. One can grow a matching pansy or viola in front of it.

A lovely shrub

I can't think why people don't grow *Hoheria Lyallii* more often, if they have a sheltered corner and want a tall 10-ft. shrub that flowers in that awkward time between late June and early July, smothered in white-and-gold flowers of the mallow family, to which the hollyhock also belongs, and sows itself in such profusion that you could have a whole forest of it if you had the leisure to prick out the seedlings and the space to replant them.

It really is a lovely thing, astonishing me every year with its profusion. I forget about it; and then there is it again with its flowers coming in their masses suggesting phila-delphus, for which it might easily be mistaken, but even more comely than any philadelphus, I think, thanks to the far prettier and paler leaf. A native of the South Island of New Zealand, it has the reputation of not being quite hardy in the colder parts of this country. That is why I said grow it in a sheltered corner. All I can tell you is that it has survived many frosty winters here in Kent (not so favour-able a climate as, say, Sussex, let alone the further western counties), including the dreadful ice-rain winter of 1946–47 and the cruel February of 1956, and that seems a good enough recommendation of character-reference for giving so lovely a thing a chance.

It has other advantages. It doesn't dislike a limy soil, always an important consideration for people who garden on chalk and can't grow any of the lime-haters. It doesn't like rich feeding, which tends to make it produce leaf rather than flower. This means an economy in compost or organic manures or inorganic fertilizers which could be better expended elsewhere. Bees love it. It is busy with bees, making their midsummer noise as you pass by.

There seems to be some confusion about what it should properly be called. I knew it first as *Plagianthus Lyallii* but now it has turned into *Hoheria Lyallii* and I am content to accept it as that. So long as a shrub gives me so much pleasure I cannot mind or bother over-much about what the botanists decide to call it. I am no botanical expert; I just know, amateurishly, what looks nice in my garden and suggests what might look equally nice in yours.

'Gipsy' roses

It is the gipsy roses that take my heart. More primly, people now call them the shrub roses, which indeed is a right and proper name for a rose that is in fact a flowering shrub, but to me they are the gipsies of the rose-tribe. They resent restraint; they like to express themselves in all their vigour freely as the fancy takes them, free as the dog-rose in the hedgerows. I know they are not to everybody's taste, and I know that it isn't everybody who has room for them in a small garden, but all the same I love them much and would sacrifice much space to them.

I wonder how many people grow a particularly charming single pink rose, well adapted for tumbling over a low wall, called *Rosa sancta*, or the Holy Rose of Abyssinia? Its name alone would justify its inclusion, and so would its history, for historically it is one of the oldest known roses and may well be the subject of a Minoan fresco at Cnossos in Crete. It has also been found woven into garlands in Egyptian tombs, so what more could any rose ask from its ancestry?

Phlox

It is a sad moment when the first phlox appears. It is the amber light indicating the end of the great burst of early summer and suggesting that we must now start looking forward to autumn. Not that I have any objection to autumn as a season, full of its own beauty; but I just cannot bear to see another summer go, and I recoil from what the first hint of autumn means.

Still, one must make up one's mind to it, and be philosophical, and make the best of what is left to us. The herbaceous phlox will do much to comfort us in the late summer and early autumn months. It does give a sumptuous glowing show, especially if you can plant it in a half-shady bed where its colours will curiously change with the sinking sun and will deepen with twilight into colours you never thought it possessed.

I feel sure that this is the way to grow phlox: in a cool, north-aspect border, all to themselves, not mixed up with other things in a hot sunny border.

They look better in isolation, closely packed; and a rather damp soil and lots of rich feeding. This means organic manure from the cowshed or pigsty if you can get it; or the indispensable bonemeal or hoof-and-horn from the shop if you can't. A mulch of peat or compost likewise provides encouragement. Anything that will keep the roots cool and will give them something to eat.

The chief enemy of the herbaceous phlox, *P. decussata*, is the small but wicked eel-worm. This is not the same brand as attacks potatoes and the bulbs of narcissus. The phlox specializes in a form of eel-worm which affects the stem and not the root. The leaves curl up and the whole plant begins to look unmistakably miserable. There is no cure unless you are prepared to use a rather dangerous remedy called *parathion*. If you are not prepared to do this, and I really wouldn't advise it for the amateur gardener, the only alternative is to cut down the infested stems *now*, and take root cuttings from your plants next April when they begin to shoot up. Thus you will get a healthy stock, free from eel-worm.

Some more roses

A rose which always catches the eye of visitors to my garden is an old Hybrid perpetual (1867) called *Baron Giraud de l'Ain*. This is a dark red rose with crinkly petals edged in white. I am not very well versed in dressmaking terms, but I am given to understand that this sort of edging is called picot in English and by the French *engrêlure*, not to be confused with *engelures*, meaning chilblains. This picot-edged rose is, in my experience, a far stronger grower than the almost indistinguishable *Roger Lambelin* (1890): Giraud seems to be blessed with a better constitution than his younger brother Roger.

Then there is the green rose. Admittedly this is a freak, and you may not like it. I don't like it very much myself; but I have a sentimental feeling for it because it grew in my old home when I was a child and one preserves a sentimental feeling for everything one knew as a child before the cares and worries of adult life came upon one. The green rose is called *Rosa chinensis viridiflora*. It makes no show in the garden, but is surprisingly decorative in a vase for picking.

One could wish only that it lived up to its name and was truly green, not tinged with brown. A jade green rose would be something worth having, but even the lovers of the so-called green rose must confess that its flowers are a bit smudgy. Either you love it, or you have no use for it; it all depends on what you feel.

The rose called *turkestanica* or *tipo ideale*, or *chinensis mutabilis* is likely to please anybody with a freakish taste. Well grown, it makes a big bush apparently smothered in several sorts of butterflies: pink, yellow and cream. It will flower all through the summer, especially if you can give it a sunny, sheltered corner. I do recommend this, if you don't already know it. It is a china with a fairly long history, and has had the honour of being drawn by Redouté.

August

More flowering shrubs

I wrote of flowering shrubs for July and August recently, but there were many that I had no space to mention. I omitted, for example, the Etna broom, *Genista aethnensis*, which always seems to astonish people and earns me a reputation that I do not at all deserve. It is no more difficult to obtain or to grow than any other broom; and if you plant it in the right place, by which I mean, in an angle against a dark background, it will display itself for several weeks in July rather like that firework known as Golden Rain, familiar to us all on village greens on the 5th of November. It is indeed a lovely thing, as light and frail as spume, pouring its mist of golden flowers from an eventual height of fifteen to twenty feet, so brilliant as to startle you when you come upon it round the corner. Do plant at least one; but insist on getting it *in a pot* from your nurseryman: it dislikes being dug up by its roots out of the ground.

I have planted hypericums under the Etna broom; they are young as yet, but will eventually flower at the same time, and I think their richer, heavier yellow will go well with the airy golden fountain overhead. These hypericums are the shrubby kind, not the ordinary low-growing St. John's Wort. They are *Hypericum patulum Henryi* and *Forrestii* for the most part, mixed with some treasured cuttings of better varieties, e.g. *H. Rowallane*, but if you just ask your nurseryman for the shrubby hypericum you

1 V. Sackville-West, with her Alsatian dog Rollo, in the garden at Sissinghurst in 1956. Her writing-room was on the first floor of the tower, which was built in about 1565.

2 This air-photograph of Sissinghurst Castle was taken in 1932, two years after Miss Sackville-West bought the property. The making of the garden had just begun but much of it was still cabbage-patches.
3 Sissinghurst in 1965. The main rose-garden lies around the circular yew hedges on the right.

The herb garden, enclosed by formal yew hedges, was the last of the small gardens to be designed, in 1938. It contains many unusual herbs like orris root, clary and woad.
Outside the herb garden is a small lawn composed entirely of thyme, *Thymus serpyllum*, which flowers at the same time as the *Iris sibirica* behind it.

6 The iris-fringed path of the rose-garden depends chiefly on old roses for its effect.
7 The main entrance to the castle, with two bronze urns from Bagatelle, near Paris, in the foreground, and a glimpse of the tower beyond.

8 The inner archway of the entrance is wreathed by the rose Allen Chandler. The Chimneys and finial date this part of the house to about 1535, but the coat-of-arms was brought from Carnock in Stirlingshire, the old seat of the Nicolson family.

9 The moat which encloses the orchard on two sides is the only relic of the mediaeval house which stood on the site of Sissinghurst Castle. An 18th-century statue of Dionysus, flanked by poplars, overlooks a mass of water-lilies.

10 Part of the box-bordered rose-garden. The rose is *Rosa villosa*.

11 A view across the moat looking, left, up the Moat Walk with its original buttressed wall facing a bank of azaleas; and, right, across the orchard to the tower. The South Cottage, made habitable in 1930, lies in the centre.

12 The lime walk, which is the main spring garden. The two borders along each side of a flagged path, shaded by pleached limes and punctuated by garden pots from Tuscany, were Harold Nicolson's particular concern. There are sheets of the blue *Anemone apennina* forget-me-nots, scillas and grape hyacinths, mixed with daffodils, erythroniums, fritillaries and *Anemone fulgens*.

13 In the White Garden. Under a silver willow-leaved pear (*Pyrus salicifolia pendula*) stands a lead statue of a virgin by the Czech sculptor Rosandic, cast from the walnut original which is also at Sissinghurst. On the right, the great metallic leaves of onopordons rise above a bed of grey *Stachys lanata*.

4 Looking through the archway from the rose-garden towards the tower lawn. The rose is Lemon Pillar.

15 The same archway shown overleaf, from the opposite direction. Beyond are the yew hedges which form the centre of the rose-garden.

6 The rose-garden (beyond the wall) seen from the top of the tower. In the centre, shaped by circular yew hedges, is the Rondel, a name given by Kentish people to the round floors of oast-houses and borrowed by them to describe this circular patch of turf.

17 The White Garden. All the flowers in this garden are white or grey. The glazed earthenware vase is Chinese, bought by Harold Nicolson in Cairo in 1937.

18 The South Cottage and Garden. V. Sackville-West's bedroom was the upper window, and Harold Nicolson's sitting-room the window below it. The border plants in this garden are mainly red, orange and yellow.

19 A tablet to the memory of V. Sackville-West, designed by Reynolds Stone, is let into the wall in the archway of the tower, beside the turret-staircase which led to her writing-room. She died at Sissinghurst on 2nd June 1962, at the age of 70.

cannot go far wrong. You will find that they will tolerate almost any ill-treatment; they will grow in shade or sun; they are most obliging, though on the whole they prefer a light soil; and for the housewife I may add that they are useful for cutting, every bud opening in water, day after day, which is a real consideration for one who has to 'do the flowers' in the house, and hasn't much time to renew fading blooms as they die.

The hydrangeas must be remembered for August; and there is *Buddleia alternifolia*, with long wands of purple, much more graceful than the common buddleia so attractive to all insects. *Clethra alnifolia*, the Sweet Pepperbush, has a tassel of white flowers with a good scent in August; not for northern gardeners but quite happy in the south.

Clerodendron Fargesii and *Clerodendron trichotomum* are stocky little trees not often seen in our gardens. Their flower is insignificant, but they are worth growing for the berries which succeed the flower. Turquoise-blue and scarlet, these clusters of berries look more like an artificial hat decoration. They are shiny, brilliantly coloured, and look as though they had been varnished. Try at least one sample in your garden. *Fargesii* is the better of the two.

A miniature herb-garden

This is not the first time I have written about herbs, and no doubt it will not be the last. My own small herb-garden is always encouragingly popular, with men as well as with the sentimentalists whom I know fatally in advance are going to say that it is full of old-world charm. Thus I make no apology for recording an excellent idea sent to me by an American correspondent. It is not arty-crafty, but severely practical, many herbs being great spreaders, whose invasion must be kept in check; and it seems to me just the thing for anybody who wants a herb-garden on a small scale, in a limited space.

You procure an old cart-wheel, the larger in diameter the better; you paint it white, with the outer rim green (where the iron tyre is), and sink the hub into a hole in the ground, so that the wheel will lie flush and level. This will give you a number of divisions in between the spokes in which to plant your herbs, plus the central hub, which you pierce through and fill with soil to grow one special, bushy little plant. (I suggest the dwarf dark purple lavender, Munstead variety.) My correspondent had fourteen divisions in which she planted chives, rue, sage, marjoram, basil, borage, balm, tansy, parsley, taragon, rosemary, thyme, pennyroyal, and sage. Personally I should have included lovage, garlic, and caraway, but obviously the choice must be left to the grower.

She sent me a coloured photograph, and the effect of the flat white wheel, white spokes, and white hub was certainly very pretty, set in grass. Set in paving stones it might be even prettier. All round the edge of the wheel, between the spokes, she had painted the appropriate names of the herbs in red. Then she had had another bright idea: behind her wheel she had sunk a semicircle of large tins with the bottoms knocked out, and in these she grew the real spreaders such as the mints, which were thus kept under control.

The Japanese anemone

At this time of the year, this dull time, this heavy August time, when everything has lost its youth and is overgrown and mature, the Japanese anemones come into flower with a queer reminder of spring. They manage, in late summer, to suggest the lightness of spring flowers. Tall, bold, stiff, they come up every year, and may indeed be regarded as a weed in the garden, so luxuriantly do they grow and increase.

The common white anemone *japonica alba* is the one best known to us all. It is a most accommodating plant in many ways, because it does not resent being grown in half shade and is not particular as to soil. Neither does it require staking. The only thing it resents is being moved. It takes at least two seasons to recover from removal; but when those two seasons have gone by, it will give you a rich return in white flowers with golden centres and a very long flowering period as bud after bud comes out. This alone makes it a satisfactory plant to grow in a shady or neglected corner where few other herbaceous plants would consent to flourish; but there are other varieties besides the common white, and it is to these that I would like to draw your attention.

The pale mauve one is, I suppose, almost as well known as the common white. It is very pretty, a lilac-mauve; but there are others, such as the variety called *Prince Henry*, a really deep mauve-pink, growing to a height of three to four feet and flowering from August to September. There are also shorter ones, growing only to one or two feet, such as *Mont Rose*, which is described as old rose in colour, and *Profusion*, purplish-red, two feet high. I must confess that I have not grown *Mont Rose* or *Profusion* and know them only by repute; but *Prince Henry* grows in my garden, in a fortunate accidental association under the wine-coloured clematis *Kermesina*. The Japanese anemone tires and droops once cut, and thus is no good for picking. But in the garden, however, it comes as a salvation in this dreary, uninteresting time of the year.

On growing lilies

A lot of people have a lot of trouble with lilies. I have myself. I try. I fail. I despair. Then I try again. Only last week did it occur to me to go and ask for advice from a famous grower of lilies in my neighbourhood, which was the obvious and sensible thing to do. I might have thought of it before. Surely he will not mind my passing on the hints he gave me, especially if it leads to an encouragement to grow some varieties of this supremely beautiful family.

There are four cardinal points, he said, like the compass. Point 1: good drainage is essential; no stagnant moisture, even if it means digging out a hole and putting a layer of crocks or coarse clinker at the bottom. Point 2: make up a suitable bed to receive your bulbs, a bed rich in humus, which means leaf-mould, peat, compost, chopped bracken, or whatever form of humus you can command. Point 3: never plant lily bulbs which have been out of the ground too long or have had their basal roots cut off. Reject these even if you find them offered at cheap rates in the horticultural department of some chain stores. Lily bulbs should be lifted fresh and replanted quickly, with their basal roots intact; therefore it is advisable to obtain them from any reputable nurseryman, who will pack them in moist peat and will never allow them to dry out before despatch. Point 4: divide when they become overcrowded.

To these hints I might add another. Most lilies dislike what professional gardeners call 'movement of air,' which in plain English means wind or a draught. I have also discovered by experience that the Regal lily, *L. regale*, likes growing amongst some covering shelter such as Southernwood (Old Man) or one of the artemisias, I suppose because the foliage gives protection to the young lily-growth against late frosts, but also because some plants take kindly to one another in association. Certainly the long white trumpets of the lily look their majestic best emerging above the grey-green cloud of these fluffy, gentle aromatic herbs.

These notes on lilies are absurdly incomplete. I thought I would amplify them next Sunday, especially because August is the month to plant the Madonna lily, the *Lilium candidum*, that virginal lily, the flower of the Annunciation, which flourishes for the cottager and often refuses to flourish in grander gardens.

The Madonna lily

Promises must be fulfilled. I said I would write something more about lilies, especially the Madonna lily, *Lilium candidum*, whose bulbs ought to be planted in this month of August. Never having grown it successfully, I am the last person to preach about it, and my remarks must be taken as theoretical.

> Where did Gabriel get a lily
> In the month of March?

I once read and have never forgotten, those two lines in a poem I have never been able to trace.* Wherever that bright Archangel found his lily, it was certainly not in the more ambitious sort of garden. It prefers the humbler home.

---

* It so happened that the author of these lines read this article and sent me the full text of the poem, which had been 'written many years ago and appeared in *Country Life*.' She has now given me permission to reprint it here.

LADY DAY

> Where did Gabriel get a lily,
> In the month of March
> When the green
> Is hardly seen

There is an old tradition that the Madonna lily throve best in cottage gardens because the housewife was in the habit of chucking out her pail of soap-suds all over the flower-bed. Curiously enough this tradition is now confirmed by the advice that the young growth of these lilies should be sprayed with a lather of soft-soap and water, to prevent the disease called botrytis. Thus do these old-wives' tales sometimes justify themselves.

The Madonna lily should be planted now without delay. There is a variety called *Salonika*, because it grows there, which is said to be more resistant to botrytis, but whichever variety you plant, put in the bulbs so shallow as to rest almost on top of the soil, showing their noses. If you bury them too deep they will have to shove themselves up in that wise way that plants have, knowing what suits them even better than we know, but this is giving them a lot of trouble and struggle which you might have spared them. So plant them shallow, and plant them as soon as they arrive; don't leave the bulbs lying about to get dry. And once planted,

---

On the early larch?
  Though I know
  Just where they grow,
I have pulled no daffodilly.
Where did Gabriel get a lily
In the month of March?
  Could I bring
  The tardy Spring
  Under Her foot's arch,
  Near or far
  The primrose star
Should bloom with violets, – willy-nilly.
  Where did Gabriel get a lily
  In the month of March?

GRACE JAMES

134

leave them alone. Don't dig them up to move them to another place. Let them stay put. They are not modern-minded, wanting to roam about; they are statically-minded; they are fond of their home, once you have induced them to take to it.

The Madonna lily is an exception to the general rule that lilies demand plenty of humus. It likes lime, which may take the form of old mortar rubble, and it likes a scratchy soil. The scratchy soil idea confirms the old theory that part of their success in cottage gardens was due to the fact that the grit from the surface of the lanes blew over the hedge and worked its way into the ground. Even to-day, when few country lanes are tarred, this may still hold good, and I have known cottagers send out their little boys with a shovel and a box mounted on old pram wheels to collect grit for the garden. It is never wise to disregard the sagacity of those who do not learn their lore from books.

Plants for shady places

People often ask what plants are suitable for a shady situation, by which they mean either the north side of a wall or house, or in the shadow cast by trees. There are so many such plants that no one need despair. A number of shrubby things will do well, such as the azaleas, the Kalmias, the rhododendrons, and a pretty, seldom seen, low-growing shrub with waxy white pendant flowers called *Zenobia pulverulenta*, always provided that the soil is lime-free for all these subjects. The many cotoneasters and berberis have no objection to shade, and are less pernickety as to soil. *Daphne laureola* will thrive, and so will *Viburnum Burkwoodii*, very easy and sweet-scented, making a big bush. The well-known Snowberry, *Symphoricarpus racemosus*, will grow anywhere and is attractive in autumn with its ivory berries and tangle of black twigs. And if you want something more choice than the Snowberry, there are many magnolias which enjoy the protection of a north wall: *M. Lennei*, wine-pink; *M. Soulangeana*, white; and *M. liliflora nigra*, a deep claret colour, which has the advantage of a very long-flowering season, all through May and June, with a few odd flowers appearing even in July and August. The magnolias all appreciate some peat or leaf-mould to fill in the hole you dig out when you plant them, and it is important not to let them suffer from drought before they have had time to become established.

If, however, you have no space for these rather large shrubs, there are plenty of things other than shrubs to fill up an un-sunny border. There are the foxgloves, which can now be obtained in varieties far superior to the woodland foxglove, flowering all round the stem, and in colours preferable to the old magenta, lovely though that may look in the woods. The hellebores and the lily-of-the-valley, the primroses and the polyanthus, the candelabra primulas, and, as you grow more ambitious, the blue poppy *Meconopsis Baileyi*, which is the dream of every gardener, will all take happily to a shaded home, especially if some moisture keeps them fresh.

West-country gardens

In the hope of picking up some new ideas, I have spent ten days visiting gardens, either famous or modest, in the West of England. My interest was concentrated on the shrubs or trees or climbers that one might find flowering at this jejune time of year.

The *indigoferas* were much in evidence, making me

wonder, as I had often wondered before, why these graceful shrubs were not more freely planted. They throw out long sprays, seven or eight feet in length, dangling with pinkish vetch-like flowers in August and September. *Indigofera Potaninii* is pale, pretty pink; *I. Gerardiana* is deeper in colour, with more mauve in it, and is perhaps the more showy of the two. They should both, I think, be planted in conjunction, so that their sprays can mingle in a cloud of the two different colours. I should like to see them combined with a front planting of a lovely new scabious, called *Grey Lady*, which I also discovered on my travels: and backed by a grey-blue clematis called *Perle d'azur*. Anyone fortunate enough to have a wall could train the clematis on that, otherwise a couple of tall poles would support it.

Three roses

A note on some roses not often seen. *Comtesse du Cayla*, a China rose, so red in the stem on young wood as to appear transparent in a bright light; very pointed in the coral-coloured bud; very early to flower, continuing to flower throughout the summer until the frosts come (I once picked a bunch on Christmas morning); somewhat romantic in her associations, for the lady in whose honour she is named was the mistress of Louis XVIII; altogether a desirable rose, not liable to black spot or mildew; needing little pruning apart from the removal of wood when it has become too old, say, every two or three years. *Mutabilis*, or *Rosa turkestanica*, makes an amusing bush, five to six feet high and correspondingly wide, covered throughout the summer with single flowers in different colours, yellow, dusky red, and coppery, all out at the same time. It is perhaps a trifle tender, and thus a sheltered corner will suit this particular harlequin.

If you want a very vigorous climber, making an incredible length of growth in one season, do try to obtain *Rosa filipes*. It is ideal for growing into an old tree, which it will quickly drape with pale-green dangling trails and clusters of small white yellow-centred flowers. I can only describe the general effect as lacy, with myriads of little golden eyes looking down at you from amongst the lace. This sounds like a fanciful description, of the kind I abhor in other writers on horticultural subjects, but really there are times when one is reduced to such low depths in the struggle to convey the impression one has oneself derived, on some perfect summer evening when everything is breathless: and one just sits, and gazes, and tries to sum up what one is seeing, mixed in with the sounds of a summer night – the young owls hissing in their nest over the cowshed, the bray of a donkey, the plop of an acorn into the pool.

Filipes means thread-like, or with thread-like stems, so perhaps my comparison to lace is not so fanciful, after all. Certainly the reticulation of the long strands overhead, clumped with the white clusters, faintly sweet-scented, always makes me think of some frock of faded green, trimmed with Point d'Alençon – or is it Point de Venise that I mean?

Dill

May I put in a good word for Dill? It is, I think, extremely pretty, both in the garden and picked for indoors, perhaps especially picked for indoors, where it looks like a very fine golden lace, feathery amongst the heavy flat heads of yarrow, *Achillea Eupatorium*, one of the most usual herbaceous plants to be found in any garden.

Dill, of course, is not an herbaceous plant; it is an annual, but it sows itself so prolifically that one need never bother about its renewal. It sees to that for itself, and comes up year after year where you want it and in many places where you don't. It has many virtues, even if you do not rely upon it 'to stay the hiccough, being boiled in wine,' or to 'hinder witches of their will.' Amongst its virtues, apart from its light yellow grace in a mixed bunch of flowers, is the fact that you can use its seeds to flavour vinegar, and for pickling cucumbers. You can also, if you wish, use the young leaves to flavour soups, sauces, and fish. All mothers know about Dill-water, but few will want to go to the trouble of preparing that concoction for themselves, so on the whole the most practical use the cook or the housewife will find for this pretty herb lies in the harvest of its seeds, which are indistinguishable from caraway seeds in seed-cake or rolled into scones or into the crust of bread. Once she has got it going in her garden, she need never fear to be short of supply for seed-cake, since one ounce is said to contain over twenty-five thousand seeds; and even if she has got a few seeds left over out of her thousand she can keep them waiting, for they will still be viable after three years.

The correct place for Dill is the herb garden, but if you have not got a herb garden it will take a very decorative place in any border. I like muddling things up; and if a herb looks nice in a border, then why not grow it there? Why not grow anything anywhere so long as it looks right where it is? That is, surely, the art of gardening.

By the way, the official botanical name of Dill is *Peucedanum graveolens*, for the information of anyone who does not prefer the short monosyllable, as I do.

Brooms

It surprises me that people should not grow the brooms more freely in their gardens. We all know the wild broom, as golden yellow as the gorse, and far more graceful, less crabbed and rebarbative; but how many of us realize that there are other varieties of startling colours to enliven our gardens in April and May?

Some of these brooms, or *Cytisus*, or Genista, really astonish in the colours they provide. You can get the garden hybrids in almost any combination you want: Venetian red, or salmon and orange, or salmon and red, or ivory and yellow, or amber and crimson, or if you want to get away from range of the hot colours, the sunset colours, you have a lavender one called Mrs. Norman Henry: and a darker one called Hookstone Purple, and a tidy little one called Lilac Time.

They are all desirable, and they should be especially valuable to people whose gardens are on a poor, hungry soil. They seem to enjoy being starved. Large lumps of manure have no attraction for them. Stones and gravel and as much sunshine as possible are what they like: but as they are most accommodating they will oblige you by growing almost anywhere within reason that you choose to set them. The only thing they appear to resent is being transplanted; so if you intend to follow my advice and order some of them for planting this coming autumn, you must insist that your nurseryman delivers them from what he will technically call ex-pots. This means that they will scarcely notice their shift from one place of growth to another.

Another point I ought to mention is that the brooms are not long-lived. After ten years or so they tend to die.

I have often extolled the virtues of *Gentiana sino-ornata*, which is beginning to flower now and should continue blooming until the end of October, but there are other late-summer-to-autumn gentians. The hybrid called *Macaulayi* is one of the best. It flowers a little earlier than *sino-ornata*, which is one of its parents, and is of the same dazzling blue, its trumpets rising from the same low-growing mat of green. Its other parent, *Farreri*, is likewise a treasure if you can obtain the true form. For those who prefer a darker blue, or who wish to combine the two shades, *Stevenagensis*, another hybrid of *sino-ornata*, is aptly described as 'shot with delphinium purple,' and its other parent, *Veitchiorum*, produces perhaps the largest trumpets of royal blue. None of these exceeds three inches in height.

Nothing could be more lovely than a great pool of them in the rock-garden. (The great pool can be achieved within a couple of years, even if you start with only a few plants, for they increase very rapidly and can be pulled to pieces and replanted in the spring.) I think that, to show them off at their best, they should be grown on a slight slope, in a pocket surrounded by stones. It is, however, essential to remember two things, namely, that they must never be allowed to suffer from drought, especially when they are making their growth, and that they will not tolerate lime in any form. You must dig out the pocket and refill it with a mixture of light leaf-mould or peat, and some sharp sand. Beware also of watering with water from the main, should you suspect any lime content; even if you do not suspect it yourself, the gentians will very soon find it out for you. Unless you are quite sure, rainwater is by far the safest.

September is the time to go to see them, in a nursery or in a private garden, and make your choice.

If you do not want to go to the trouble of preparing a leafy bed, *Gentiana septemfida*, August flowering, somewhat taller, and of a very dark blue, is less particular as to soil and will grow almost anywhere. Then if you are so fortunate as to possess a damp, boggy place, the Willow Gentian, *G. asclepiadea*, will grow for you into great blocks of blue, a foot and a half in height, and rather untidy, so that the ideal place for it is the wild garden. Any place where primulas thrive will suit it, and it is one of those useful things which are happy with a certain amount of shade. There is also a white form, less attractive in my opinion. *G. Makinoi* is another which prefers moisture; this is sturdier and less floppy than the Willow Gentian, and has the additional merit of turning its leaves red in autumn.

I do not think, however, that any of these coarser gentians has the charm of the flat carpeting dwarfs, finger-high, which combine delicacy with brilliance just at the time of year when one wants them most.

Docteur Jamain and some others

Whatever differences of opinion we may hold about roses, and whether our taste inclines to the hybrid teas, or to the ramblers or to the old shrub roses, there is one thing on which we are all in agreement: it is an advantage for a rose to smell like a rose. The accusation is often brought against what people loosely call 'modern roses' that they have lost their scent, an accusation sometimes but not always justified. *Charles Mallerin*, for instance, that magnificent black-red hybrid tea, dates back only ten years and is as rich in scent as it is in colour. I recall also, and still grow, a huge pink climber called *Colcestria* which won the competition for the best-scented rose somewhere back in the 1920's; I cannot find it listed in any catalogue now, which seems a pity as it is not only powerfully scented but is what nurserymen describe as 'vig.' I must try to propagate it.

There are roses which are 'fast of their scent', requiring to be held to the nose, and others which generously spread themselves upon the summer air. Of these, I would signal three in particular: *Rosa rugosa alba* and *rugosa Blanc Double de Coubert*, and the hybrid musk *Penelope*. These all make big bushes, and should be placed near a corner where you frequently pass. They all have the merit of continuous flowering, and *rugosa alba* produces bright red hips in autumn, like little round apples amongst the yellowing leaves, adding to its attraction, interest and charm.

The rugosa hybrid, *Parfum de l'Hay*, has the reputation of being one of the most strongly scented of all roses. Unfortunately its constitution is not as strong as its scent. Perhaps light soils don't suit it. Its companion, *Roseraie de l'Hay*, might do better, and smells nearly as good. Neither of them makes a big bush, so would be suitable for a small garden.

Souvenir du Docteur Jamain is an old hybrid perpetual which I am rather proud of having rescued from extinction. I found him growing against the office wall of an old nursery. No one knew what he was; no one seemed to care; no one knew his name; no one had troubled to propagate him. Could I dig him up? I asked. Well, if you like to risk it, they said, shrugging their shoulders; it's a very old plant, with a woody stiff root. I risked it; *Docteur Jamain* survived his removal; and now has a flourishing progeny in my garden and also on the market of certain rosarians to whom I gave him. *Docteur Jamain* is a deep red, not very large flowers, but so sweetly and sentimentally scented. Some writers would call it nostalgically scented, meaning everything that burying one's nose into the heart of a rose meant in one's childhood, or in one's adolescence when one first discovered poetry, or the first time one fell in love.

I think *Docteur Jamain* should not be planted in too sunny a place. He burns. A south-west aspect suits him better than full south.

Making garden-notes

If you have acquired the habit of always carrying a pencil and note-book, this is a good time to jot down some effects of light on a summer evening.

It is of course obvious that one should set plants designed for autumn-colour in a place where the sun will strike them. Everybody knows that. Maples and so on. But I do suggest to you that during this August holiday you might walk round your garden and notice the variation of light in our latening summer months, and record in a note-book the things you have observed. One says too easily, Oh, I shall remember that! and then time passes and one no longer remembers, and one tries to think back to that August evening when one knew there was something one intended to remember, but the vision has gone: and next year has come, and no record remains unless you have carried a pencil and a note-book always in your pocket.

Rosa alba

I will now write about *Rosa alba*. This sounds as though it were invariably a white rose. Make no mistake. The adjective is misleading. Although it is true that *Rosa alba semi-plena* may have been the White Rose of York, and *alba maxima* the Great Double White or Jacobite rose, the alba roses include many forms which are not white but pink. The old Maiden's Blush of cottage gardens is an alba; the French called it *Cuisse de Nymphe*, and when it appeared in an even rosier variant they called it *Cuisse de Nymphe Emue*. We, in our Puritanical England, acknowledge no truck with the thighs of nymphs, however emotional, so under the name of Maiden's Blush it remains, and a very pretty and innocent-looking pink and white débutante she is.

There are other alba roses which make my delight. Sometimes I think that *alba Celestial* is one of the loveliest shrubs one could ever wish to contemplate, with its shell-pink flowers amongst its grey-green leaves. Then I look up into the tall bush of *Queen of Denmark* and think that she is possibly even more lovely, in a deeper pink than *alba Celestial*, with a quartered flower looking as though someone had taken a spoon and stirred it round, as a child might stir a bowl of strawberries and cream.

Mr. Edward Bunyard, who did so much to restore the historical roses to favour and circulation, was of the opinion that the albas were very useful in many unusual ways. They would tolerate difficult situations, thriving in soil penetrated by the roots of trees (he instances woodland walks); he claimed that they were resistant to mildew; and added that they could either be pruned or left unpruned, according to the taste of the grower, the space available, and the time that could be devoted to them. Mr. Graham Thomas, whose book *The Old Shrub Roses* I am constantly recommending, goes even further. According to him, they are resistant to all diseases; enjoy such vigour and longevity as to survive neglect for a hundred years; will grow in damp, cold, north-country gardens; and can successfully be planted against a north wall. Unlike Mr. Bunyard, however, he recommends that they should be closely pruned, in December or January, leaving the long shoots at one-third of their length, so between these two authorities we can take our choice and make our own experiments as to pruning.

More for your rose-garden

If you were born with a romantic nature, all roses must be crammed with romance, and if a particular rose originated on an island the romance must be doubled, for an island is romantic in itself.

The island I refer to lies off the south-east coast of Africa, near Mauritius. It used to be called the Ile Bourbon, now called Réunion. The inhabitants of this small island had the pleasing habit of using roses for their hedges: only two kinds, the Damask rose and the China rose. These two married in secret; and one day, in 1817, the curator of the botanic garden on the Ile Bourbon noticed a seedling he transplanted and grew on, a solitary little bastard which has fathered or mothered the whole race we now call the Bourbon roses.

It is curious to find Mr. Edward Bunyard writing in 1936 in his book *Old Garden Roses* that the Bourbon roses 'are now almost forgotten,' and listing only four as being 'still obtainable.' (*Hermosa*, *Bourbon*, *Louise Odier*, and *Mme Pierre Oger*.) He does not even mention *Zéphyrine Drouhin*, the rose which so far back as 1868 decided to discard armaments and has been known as the Thornless rose ever since. This shows how taste has changed within the last twenty years, for it is now possible to obtain at least two dozen different varieties.

Far from being forgotten, now that the shrub roses have returned to favour, *Rosa bourboniana* includes some of the most desirable. Their scent alone makes one realize the extent to which they have inherited that quality from their damask parent; one has only to think of *Mme Isaac Péreire* and *Mme Pierre Oger*, admittedly two of the most fragrant roses in cultivation. We all have our scented favourites; and someone is bound to say, 'What about *Parfum de l'Hay?*,' but I must still support the claim of these two ladies in the Bourbon group.

The cross has resulted in an oddly varied lot. There is *Coupe de Hebé*, 1840, which you might easily mistake for a centifolia or cabbage rose; and if you like the striped roses there are *Honorine de Brabant* and *Commandant Beaurepaire*, 1874, pink and white like *Rosa mundi*, but not, I contend, as good as that ancient Rose of the World. Among the more recent crosses, *Zigeuner Knabe*, 1909, makes the most swagger boastful bush you could set at any corner: a reddish purple, it looks more like a Cardinal fully robed, about to set off in procession, than like the *Gypsy Boy* we call it in English.

Bourbon roses

Among the Bourbon roses, lack of space compelled me to omit *Mme Lauriol de Barny*, and indeed she is very large and proud. At a distance, but for the foliage, you might mistake her for a small peony. (I am aware that the French do not recognize her as a true Bourbon, but classify her under the curious name of hybrid *non-remontant*.) Dating back to 1868, she has all the rosy lavishness of ladies of the Second Empire. I wish I could find out who Mme Lauriol was in real life, to have so sumptuous a flower called after her. I suspect that she may have belonged to the *haute cocottierie* of Paris at that date, or possibly I misjudge her and she may have been the perfectly respectable wife of some M. de Barny, perhaps a rose-grower at Lyon. Someone ought to write the biographies of persons who have had roses named in their honour. Who was Mme Hardy? Who was Charles de Mills? I don't know, and I long for a Who's Who to correct my ignorance.

Souvenir de la Malmaison, 1843, is easier to place as to name, although Josephine Beauharnais can never have seen it. I suppose there will be screams if I say that this famous rose has never been one of my favourites. A perfect bloom, yes; but how often do we get one? It all too easily goes brown and sodden. The best thing I have to say for it is that it played its part in producing *Gloire de Dijon*, that fragrant crumpled straw-coloured old stager, equally charming as a climber or as a bush. *Variegata di Bologna* is a fairly recent production, 1909, and is said to be a strong grower on rich soils. It looks miserable in my garden, greatly to my regret, for I know of no other rose with its colouring: violet stripes on a white background. Mr. Graham Thomas suggests that it might do well under a north-west wall, with a cool root-run. No doubt I have planted it in too sunny a place.

This does not by any means exhaust the list of the Bourbon roses. I have omitted *La Reine Victoria*, who appeared in 1872, although I have mentioned her child, *Mme Pierre Oger*. *Mme E. Calvat* I have never seen, but know by repute as one of the best, pink and scented, and suitable for growing up a pillar. *Roi des pourpres*, now renamed *Prince Charles*, is not to my mind amongst the best of the violet or lilac roses; for this colour I would rather go to *Cardinal Richelieu*, a gallica, or *William Lobb*, a moss. Finally, *Blairi No. 2* is a most exquisite climber, rather a deep pink; I believe that its somewhat unexpected name is due to the fact that the

Mr. Blair who raised it and others in 1845 could not be bothered to find appropriate names for them all.

The Bourbon roses should not be heavily pruned, and indeed their full beauty can be displayed only when they are allowed to grow into the great tall bushes natural to them. Dead and twiggy wood should be cut out. How easy to say, and how scratchy to do.

Acacias

There are few summer-flowering trees prettier than acacias, when they hang out their pale, sweet-scented tassels, and few faster of growth for people in a hurry. Their correct name is *Robinia pseudoacacia*, but as acacia is the current usage I let it stand. They abound in France and Italy, but are equally at home with us. I have planted them no taller than a walking-stick, and within a contemptible number of years they have taken on the semblance of an established inhabitant, with sizeable trunks and a rugged bark and a spreading head, graceful and fringy. If they have a fault, it is that their boughs are brittle, that they make a good deal of dead wood, and, I suspect, are not very long-lived, especially if the main trunk has forked, splitting the tree into halves. This danger can be forestalled by allowing only one stem to grow up, with no subsidiary lower branches.

If, after reading this cautionary tale, you still decide to plant an acacia, let me suggest that you might try not only the ordinary white-flowered one, but also the lovely pink one, *Robinia hispida*, the rose acacia. It is no more expensive to buy than the white, and is something less often seen, a surprise to people who expect white flowers and suddenly see pink. *Robinia Kelseyi* is another rose-pink form much to be recommended.

September

Wall-climbers

The two great planting months, October and November, are close upon us, and those gardeners who desire the maximum of reward with the minimum of labour would be well advised to concentrate upon the flowering shrubs and flowering trees. How deeply I regret that fifteen years ago, when I was forming my own garden, I did not plant these desirable objects in sufficient quantity. They would by now be large adults instead of the scrubby, spindly infants I contemplate with impatience as the seasons come round.

That error is one from which I would wish to save my fellow-gardeners, so, taking this opportunity, I implore them to secure trees and bushes from whatever nurseryman can supply them: they will give far less trouble than the orthodox herbaceous flowers, they will demand no annual division, many of them will require no pruning; in fact, all that many of them will ask of you is to watch them grow yearly into a greater splendour, and what more could be exacted of any plant?

Your choice will naturally depend upon the extent of your garden, but it should be observed that any garden, however small, has a house in it, and that that house has walls. This is a very important fact to be remembered. Often I hear people say, 'How lucky you are to have these old walls; you can grow anything against them,' and then, when I point out that every house means at least four walls –

north, south, east, and west – they say, 'I never thought of that.' Against the north and west sides you can grow magnolias or camellias; on the east side, which catches the morning sun, you can grow practically any of the hardy shrubs or climbers, from the beautiful ornamental quinces, commonly, though incorrectly, called Japonicas (the right name is Cydonia, or even more correctly, Chaenomeles,) to the more robust varieties of *Ceanothus*, powdery-blue, or a blue fringing on purple. On the south side the choice is even larger – a vine, for instance, will soon cover a wide, high space, and in a reasonable summer will ripen its bunches of small, sweet grapes (I recommend Royal Muscadine, if you can get it); or, if you want a purely decorative effect, the fast-growing *Solanum crispum*, which is a potato though you might not think it, will reach to the eaves of the house and will flower in deep mauve for at least two months in early summer.

And apart from these wall-plants, many small trees may be set in convenient places. The flowering cherries and crabs have fortunately become a feature of most gardens, and how gaily they contribute to the aspect of English villages and cottages during the spring. Many of them, however, tend towards a rather crude pink; and those who would wish to avoid this colour may be better advised to plant the subtler greenish-white cherry called Ukon (*Cerasus Lannesiana grandiflora*) or the white-blossomed crab *Dartmouth*, with purplish-red fruits of remarkable beauty in the autumn; or that other crab, *Niedzwetzkyana*, with even more beautiful purple fruits. The almond, of course, will always be a favourite, partly because it flowers so early in the year; but if you are thinking of planting almonds now I would strongly recommend the variety called *Pollardii*, with a finer and deeper flower than the common kind usually seen.

The advantage of trees and shrubs is that they may be underplanted with bulbs – another activity which should not be neglected at this time of year. Daffodils, narcissi, and hyacinths should be got into the ground without delay. Bulbs are always a good investment, as they increase underground and may be lifted yearly, and the little offsets or bulbils planted out in a spare corner to develop. Such raising of one's own stock is much more satisfying than writing a cheque or buying a postal order.

Rather rare

For two or three years past I have been trying to run to earth a plant called *Tropaeolum polyphyllum*, a native of Chile. 'Run to earth' is indeed the right phrase, for it buries itself so deep in the ground that it is impossible to dig up. All efforts to obtain a tuber from the garden of a friend, where it grows like a weed, proved vain; it simply snapped off, and for all I know the essential tuber was half-way down between Kent and the Antipodes. Now, however, in one week, I have found it advertised by two separate nurserymen, one of whom remarks that 'for some reason it has become rather rare.'

It should not be allowed to become rare, for it is a very showy, decorative thing, flowering in June, in long creeping trails of bright yellow nasturtium-like trumpets extending nearly a yard long from its grey-green leaves. I cannot improve upon the description given by one of the nurserymen listing it: 'It makes a wonderful effect with its glaucous foliage and garlands of blossom.' It certainly does. It looks like golden serpents writhing out of a sea-green base. The ideal place to plant it, I imagine, would be in a dry wall, say in some Cotswold garden, when it could tuck its roots into cool crevices and could allow its garlands of blossom to pour in golden waterfalls down some small vertical cliff of that lovely stone. Alternatively it would look well in a rock garden, for it seems to demand stone to set it off, and thus is not so suitable for a bed or border.

The moral of its preference for deep rooting is to plant it deep at the outset, at least a foot to eighteen inches. I imagine that like its relation *Tropaeolum speciosum*, the flame-coloured nasturtium which does so brilliantly in Scotland and so poorly in England, it would not object to partial shade. Do not be alarmed when it disappears entirely during the winter: it will reappear in spring. It also has the pleasant habit of rambling about through anything which may be planted near it, and of coming up in unexpected places.

A useful clematis flowering in September is *Clematis flammula*. I would not advocate it for an important or prominent place, as its masses of small white flowers are not in the least showy, but for scrambling over a rough shed or outhouse, where its peculiarly musty scent may be caught by the passer-by. Its great virtue is that it will flourish in places which never get any sun, the picture of contentment on a cruelly dark north wall. There is a pale pink variety, which might be more pleasing, but I cannot speak from experience.

Rosemary

It surprises me always when people fail to recognize the common rosemary. 'What is that?' they say, looking at the great dark-green bushes that sprawl so generously over the paths at the entrance to the place where I live. I should have thought that rosemary was one of our most common plants, if only for the sake of its sentimental associations. It was said to have the peculiar property of strengthening the memory, and thus became a symbol of fidelity for lovers. 'A sprig of it hath a dumb language,' said Sir Thomas More; and another legend connects it with the age of Our Lord, thirty-three years, after which it stops growing in height but never in width. A romantic plant, yet so oddly, it seems, unknown.

There are several different forms of rosemary. There is the ordinary bush type, *Rosmarinus officinalis*, which can be grown either as a bush or clipped into shape as a hedge. I don't like it so well as a hedge, because the constant clipping means the loss of the flowers which are half its beauty, but all the same it makes a dense neat hedge if you want one. Do not cut back into the old wood. Then there is the Corsican rosemary, *R. angustifolius Corsicus* with a more feathery growth of leaf and bright blue flowers, almost gentian blue; it is less tough-looking than the common rosemary, and perhaps not quite so hardy, but so lovely a thing that it well deserves a sheltered corner. It hates cold winds. The fastigiate or pyramidal rosemary, pleasingly called *Miss Jessup's Upright*, will make sentinels six feet high within a couple of years. (Who was Miss Jessup, I wonder?) There is also a creeping form, suitable for rock-gardens, called *prostratus*, but this is not very hardy and I would not recommend it to anybody not living in the warmer counties. If it can be persuaded to thrive, however, as it might be induced to do with its roots sheltering a long way back between stones, away from frost and damp, it makes a grateful mat of evergreen and a good covering plant for little early bulbs coming up through it, such as the Lady Tulip, *T. Clusiana*, or the jonquils, or the miniature narcissi such as *N. juncifolius*, so sweet scented.

It should not be forgotten, either, that a white-flowered form of the common rosemary is obtainable, making a change from the blue-flowered form more usually seen.

Most of the rosemaries will flourish anywhere in the sun, preferring a light soil, even a poor sandy stony soil, and will root very easily from cuttings taken off in September, stuck firmly into sand, and left to grow on until next spring when they can be planted out.

Low Alpines

A most pleasing and original suggestion reaches me in a nurseryman's catalogue. It is the sort of suggestion which could provide extra colour and interest in a small garden, without taking up too much space and without involving too much labour. It is, simply, the idea of growing low Alpines in a narrow border on both sides of the path running from your gate to your door, or, of course, on both sides or even one side of any path you may find suitable.

By 'low' Alpines I do not mean those plants which occur only on the lower slopes of mountains, a technical term in horticulture, as opposed to the 'high' Alpines. I mean flat-growing; close to the ground; the sorts that make little tufts and squabs and cushions and pools of colour when in flower, and neat tight bumps of grey or green for the rest of the year when the flowers have gone over. The range of choice is wide. Saxifrages, silene, stonecrops, thrift, Raoulia, acaena, androsace, aubretia in moderation, thyme, *Achillea argentea, Erinus alpinis, Tunica saxifraga, Morisia hypogaea, Bellis Dresden China*, sempervivum or houseleeks, some campanulas such as *C. garganica*, so easy and self-sowing – the list is endless, and gives scope for much variety.

I would not restrict it only to the rugs and mats and pillows, but would break its level with some inches of flower-stalks, such as the orange Alpine poppy, *Papaver alpinum*, and some violas such as *V. gracilis* or *V. bosnaica*, and some clumps of dianthus such as the Cheddar pink or the prettily named Dad's Favourite, and even some primroses specially chosen, such as *rosea* or *Garriard Ganymede* or *Betty Green*, and any other favourite which may occur to you. This list is not intended to dictate. It is intended only to suggest that a ribbon or band of colour, no more than twelve inches wide, might well wend its flat way beside a path in even the most conventional garden.

But if you had a garden on a slope, in a hilly district, what an opportunity would be yours! Then your flat ribbon would become a rill, a rivulet, a beck, a burn, a brook, pouring crookedly downhill between stones towards the trout-stream flowing along the valley at the bottom. I suppose some people do possess gardens like that, in Gloucestershire for instance, or in Cumberland, or in the Highlands. Let those fortunate ones take notice, and, dipping an enormous paint-brush into the wealth offered by the autumn catalogues, splash its rainbow result wherever their steps may lead them.

Planting in masses

The more I see of other people's gardens the more convinced do I become of the value of good grouping and shapely training. These remarks must necessarily apply most forcibly to gardens of a certain size, where sufficient space is available for large clumps or for large specimens of individual plants, but even in a small garden the spotty effect can be avoided by massing instead of dotting plants here and there.

It is a truly satisfactory thing to see a garden well schemed and wisely planted. Well schemed are the operative words. Every garden, large or small, ought to be planned from the outset, getting its bones, its skeleton, into the shape that it will preserve all through the year even after the flowers have faded and died away. Then, when all colour has gone, is the moment to revise, to make notes for additions, and even to take the mattock for removals. This is gardening on the large scale, not in details. There can be no rules, in so fluid and personal a pursuit, but it is safe to say that a sense of substance and solidity can be achieved only by the presence of an occasional mass breaking the more airy companies of the little flowers.

What this mass shall consist of must depend upon many things: upon the soil, the aspect, the colour of neighbouring plants, and above all upon the taste of the owner. I can imagine, for example, a border arranged entirely in purple and mauve – phlox, stocks, pansies, clematis Jackmanii trained over low hoops – all planted in bays between great promontories of the plum-coloured sumach, *Rhus cotinus foliis purpureis*, but many people, thinking this too mournful, might prefer a scheme in red and gold. It would be equally easy of accomplishment, with a planting of the feathery *Thalictrum glaucum*, gaillardias, *Achillea eupatorium* (the flat-headed yellow yarrow), *Helenium*, *Lychnis chalcedonica*, and a host of other ordinary, willing, herbaceous things. In this case, I suppose, the mass would have to be provided by bushes of something like the golden privet or the golden yew, both of which I detest when planted as 'specimens' on a lawn, but which in so aureate a border would come into their own.

The possibilities of variation are manifold, but on the main point one must remain adamant; the alternation between colour and solidity, decoration and architecture, frivolity and seriousness. Every good garden, large or small, must have some architectural quality about it; and, apart from the all-important question of the general lay-out, including hedges, the best way to achieve this imperative effect is by massive lumps of planting such as I have suggested.

I wish only that I could practise in my own garden the principles which I so complacently preach, week after week, in this column.

Some reminders

Writing away from home, I make a few notes of things seen in the course of a fortnight's motoring, things which were either new to me, or else forgotten until the reminder came along. I had forgotten, for instance, the summer-flowering mauve *Solanum crispum* var. *autumnalis*, so useful in August, a trifle tender, perhaps, wanting a warm south wall; and the white *Solanum jasminoides*, another August flowerer: a most graceful climber, also a trifle tender, but well worth trying in southern counties. I had forgotten the white – or, rather, creamy – *Buddleia Fallowiana alba*, with grey leaves, an uncommon thing and a pleasant change from the ordinary mauve. *Buddleia nivea* is even more grey-leaved and woolly, almost as woolly and felted as that old favourite cottage plant, *Stachys lanata*, commonly called Rabbit's Ears or Saviour's Flannel, or, in Scotland, Lamb's Lugs. I had forgotten *Itea ilicifolia*, a wall shrub with long, grey-white catkins of soft beauty, an evergreen, fragrant and, alas tender; and *Berberis trifoliata*, expressly made to appeal to anyone with a liking for glaucous foliage.

Then I saw also a shrubby plant which I was later enabled to identify as *Abelia grandiflora*. This struck me as a surprisingly pretty shrub; it throws a wealth of pointed, bright pink buds, opening into pink-white flowers. It is quite hardy, and I would recommend it to anyone who wants some colour in the August–September garden.

Another shrub I saw was *Decaisnea Fargesii*. This is called the bean-plant, because it develops bright-blue seed-pods in autumn; very decorative. It is quite hardy and should be planted in any unwanted corner, just for the sake of its yellow-green flowers and its steel-blue pods in autumn.

These are all just notes; but I must end by urging you to grow *Indigofera pendula*. This is a surprisingly lovely thing. It arches in long sprays of pinkish-mauve pea-like flowers, growing ten feet high, dangling very gracefully from its delicate foliage. It combines very prettily with the mauve Solanum I mentioned above; or, I can imagine, with the August-flowering blue Ceanothus, *Gloire de Versailles*, or even mingling with the blue plumbago, *Ceratostigma Willmottiana*.

Peat-walls

I would like to suggest the still somewhat novel idea of constructing low, dry-walls out of blocks of peat. It is a method which will probably appeal most to the advanced or advancing gardener whose ambition is to grow small choosey plants which abhor lime and demand an utterly acid soil.

You build your wall, which can be anything from two to four courses high, setting each course a few inches back from the one below, and then fill in the space behind it with a rich mixture of well-rotted leaf mould, peat, and bone meal. Remember that this will sink at first, so keep a supply for filling up. If you have no bank against which to prop your wall, you could, if you liked, build in the form of a square, a circle or a rectangle, thus giving yourself the advantage of a wall-aspect to every point of the compass, adapted to plants requiring full sun or a cooler situation. The *Ramondas*, for instance, should always be grown facing north; the gentians enjoy a half-way house, sunny for part of the day, but not too merciless.

You then proceed to the exciting moment of setting your plants. As you will probably have obtained them out of pots from a nurseryman, when some of them may be in flower, you will have the rare pleasure of getting an effect straight away, and moreover will be enabled to move them about before the actual planting, to study colour effects and harmonies.

What you plant must naturally depend upon your personal wishes, but I would suggest a generous proportion of the autumn-flowering gentians, whose blue trumpets varying from Cambridge to Oxford show up to great advantage against the dark background of peat. *Lithospermum Grace Ward*, a trailing plant of an equally intense blue, is in flower for practically the whole summer, and should certainly be allowed to hang freely over the wall-face. *Mertensia echioides* in a cool place is likewise blue in summer; and some of the smaller primulas such as *frondosa* and *farinosa*, with their mealy grey rosettes of leaves and tiny pink heads, would look charming in little groups at intervals.

The well-known *Primula rosea*, of a deeper pink, should soon develop into clumps; and the lilac *P. marginata*, with its curiously sawlike leaves, should provide a variation in colour. If you were more ambitious, you could try a few *Primula Vialii*, which rise to a height of 15 in. or so, and carry most striking flower-heads, pointed like a Welsh-woman's hat in red and purple instead of black.

On the flat top I think some dwarf shrubs would make an interesting contrast. Here, again, it must be according to taste. There are low-growing azaleas and rhododendrons; there is the large family of *ericas* or heaths; there is the delightful *Andromeda polyfolia compacta*, not a foot high, like a miniature Kalmia, each separate bloom like a minute chintz sun-bonnet; there is a lovely spring-flowering shrub most unfairly saddled with the name *Menziesia ciliicalyx lasiophylla*, a very deep rose in the flower and a good autumn colourer; there is *Gaulnettya Wisley Pearl*, white-flowered in spring and red-berried later on; and finally I might suggest *Daphne Blagayana*, a great favourite of mine, partly on account of its strong, sweet scent.

This will send out long woody shoots from the centre, and these should be pegged down or held down by stones after making a slanting cut in the stem where it is to be pressed into the soil, when it will eventually form a starfish of a clump, several feet in circumference.

Layering

I recommend the pegging-down of *Daphne Blagayana*, a plant which indeed exacts such treatment or it will soon deteriorate, and this put me in mind of the satisfactory pleasure of this method of propagation. I suppose every grower of carnations at one time or another has secured their side shoots into a mould of sand with strong hairpins; but it is perhaps not generally realized by the amateur gardener how many shrubs and climbers will lend themselves happily to layering. It is possible to obtain quite a nursery of young, rooted stock in a short time, at no cost and for very little trouble.

Layering can be done at any time, though autumn and spring are the best. More dependable than cuttings, some proportion of which must always fail save in the most expert hands, layers are almost bound to take root. As I said in the case of *Daphne Blagayana*, you make a slanting cut in the stem where it is to be inserted into the soil, and then cover it over with earth and hold it down by means of a brick or heavy bit of stone. Best of all is to sink a flower-pot filled with good soil and press the layer into that. By this means, when the time comes for the rooted layer to be separated from the parent plant, usually about a year, the pot can be lifted out of the ground with no disturbance to its occupant, a particularly valuable point in the case of plants which resent disturbance, such as the clematis.

Honeysuckles sometimes layer themselves of their own accord, so avail yourselves of the hint if you want to increase your supply. Azaleas are commonly propagated by layering, but it takes some time to get a young plant of decent size. Sometimes it is not practicable to bend a shoot down to meet the ground without snapping it off, and this difficulty may be overcome by raising a pot to the required height, on an old wooden box, for instance, but be careful not to let the pot dry out. This is the easiest method for propagating magnolias, whose side branches generally start rather high up the trunk and are apt to be too brittle to be very flexible.

I think the first shrub to draw my attention to its self-layering propensity was the Allspice, or Sweet Bush, *Caly-*

canthus occidentalis and *C. floridus*, botanically related to the Wintersweet. This is such a useful thing for a sunny place, as it starts producing its brown-red flowers in June and goes on doing so right into September. Of the two I like *C. occidentalis* the better, because although it is rather more straggly in its growth than *floridus*, the flowers are redder and the leaves more aromatic when crushed. The wood also is extremely aromatic. I do not know why it should be called Allspice, whose proper name is *Pimenta officinalis*, a greenhouse plant in this country, whereas the two Americans are perfectly hardy in the open. They like a loamy soil, and I should add the cautionary remark that they are said to be poisonous to cattle.

Campions

I once observed a brilliant showy plant growing in the prettiest of Scottish nursery gardens, Inshriarch, near Aviemore. I long to go back there. The garden had been carved out of a clearing in a wood of silver birch and dark green juniper; many little burns ran down channels cut in the peaty soil; primulas and gentians grew like weeds, though true weeds there were none. It was not only the prettiest but also the tidiest of nursery gardens, crammed with covetable things which I feared I could not grow with any success down here in the south-east of England.

I did, however, bring away a pot-grown plant of *Lychnis haageana*, the showy brilliant plant I referred to; and it has served me well. I would recommend it to everybody who wants a flare of colour for the front of the border or for the rock garden in July. I saved its seed, but need scarcely have troubled to do so, as it came up of its own accord in unexpected places, a most agreeable device for a plant which, although nominally a perennial, is apt to die out after a year or so. My original plant hasn't, yet, but has left so profuse a progeny that its departure into another world would not now matter, except that one is always sorry to say good-bye.

This would be the time to obtain ripe seed for sowing. I must warn prospective growers that this campion, the English name for lychnis, is variable when you grow it from seed. The seed I saved and sowed threw flowers in different colours. Some of them came in the bright orange red of the flame of an oil-lamp, *lychnos* being the Greek word for a lamp. Some of them came much paler, straw-coloured; some came pale pink; and some a dull white. I scrapped the white; threw them out; kept the straw-coloured and the pink and left the rest to seed themselves and take a chance on their coming up in the show they will make, as I hope next year.

They are rather untidy; their leaves are ugly; their flowers shaggy and tattered like a flag torn in a gale. But so gay, even as a flag flying 12 in. above the ground.

Truly, they are worth this recommendation. They got an Award of Merit from the R.H.S. in 1953, which is something worth having, a more valuable sanction than I could give.

Campions all, they belong to the same family as the Ragged Robin of our banks and woodlands, and as the tall, scarlet, rather coarse *Lychnis chalcedonica* so familiar once in old herbaceous borders and still not to be despised.

Ulrich Brunner and some others

The Bourbon roses gave birth to the race of hybrid perpetuals, who in their turn were developed into the hybrid teas. The hybrid perpetuals have now become somewhat obsolete and superseded by the hybrid teas, a pity in my opinion since there are still some H.P.'s available and some of them are very useful for prolonging the season besides having the quality as lasting well in water. This is especially true of *Ulrich Brunner*, stiff-stemmed, almost thornless, cherry-red in colour, very prolific indeed, a real cut-and-come-again.

These strong growers lend themselves to various ways of treatment. They can be left to reach their free height of 7 to 8 ft., but then they wobble about over eye-level and you can't see them properly, with the sun in your eyes, also they get shaken by summer gales. A better but more laborious system is to tie them down to benders, by which I mean flexible wands of hazel with each end poked firmly into the ground and the rose-shoots tied down at intervals, making a sort of half-hoop. This entails a lot of time and trouble, but is satisfactory if you can do it; also it means that the rose breaks at each joint, so that you get a very generous *floraison*, a lovely word I should like to see imported from the French into our language. If you decide to grow hybrid perpetuals on this system of pegging them down, you ought to feed them richly, with organic manure if you can get it, or with compost if you make it, but anyhow with something that will compensate for the tremendous effort they will put out from being encouraged to break all along their shoots. You can't ask everything of a plant, any more than you can exact everything of a human being, without giving some reward in return. Even the performing seal gets an extra herring.

Ulrich Brunner, Frau Karl Druschki, and the Dicksons, Hugh and George, are very suitable for this kind of training.

The hybrid perpetuals can also be used as wall plants; not nearly so tall as true climbers and ramblers, they are quite tall enough for, say, a space under a ground floor window; or they may be grown on post-and-wire as espaliers outlining a path. I once had a blood-red Dickson trained in the shape of a peacock's tail.

I find *Paul Neyron* described in one rosarian's catalogue as having 'the largest flowers we know among roses ... suffused with an exquisite shade of lilac, with silver reverse,' and in another catalogue as having 'enormous rich pink flowers, fully double.' This sounds all right to me; I have long since learnt not to be misled by catalogue descriptions, but these are from two catalogues that I can trust. Moreover, *Paul Neyron* appears to be identical with, or indistinguishable from, the famous Rose de la Reine, raised in 1840 by M. Laffay, of Auteuil, who grew 200,000 seedling roses a year and took his chance of finding something really good amongst them.

The rambling wichurianas are especially suited for growing up old trees, since with one or two exceptions such as *Albertine* and *Alberic Barbier* they are apt to develop mildew on a wall, and prefer the air to blow freely through them. *Félicité et Perpétue*, commemorating two young women who suffered martyrdom at Carthage in A.D. 203, will grow at least 20 ft. high into the branches, very appropriately, since St. Perpetua was vouchsafed the vision of a wonderful ladder reaching up to heaven. *François Juranville* and *Léontine Gervais*, both pink-and-buff, hang prettily, if less vigorous of growth. Among other wichurianas, of a stiffer character than the ramblers, *The New Dawn* and *Dr. Van Fleet* are to my mind two of the best, very free-flowering throughout the summer, of a delicate but definite rose-pink. *Emily Gray*, reputed tender though I have never found her so, planted on a south-facing wall, large single pale yellow flowers, and dark green shiny leaves; *Cupid*, a hybrid tea, pink with a gold central boss; and *Elegance*, white and gold, are all very much to be recommended. *Mermaid* is perhaps too well known to be mentioned, but should never be forgotten, partly for the sake of the pale-yellow flowers, opening flat and single, and partly because of the late flowering season, which begins after most other climbers are past their best. I must add that *Mermaid* should be regarded with caution by dwellers in cold districts.

Where the choice is so wide it becomes difficult to include all that certainly deserve inclusion, but I must mention *Allen Chandler*, a magnificent red, only semi-double, which carries some bloom all through the summer. Not, I think, a rose for a house of new brick, but superb on grey stone, or on white-wash, or indeed any colour-wash. If you want a white rose, flushed pink, scented, very vigorous and seldom without flowers, try *Mme Alfred Carrière*, best on a sunny wall but tolerant of a west or even a north aspect; and if a yellow rose, very deep yellow, plant *Lawrence Johnston*, of which it must, however, be said that the first explosion of bloom is not usually succeeded by many subsequent flowers.

Finally, remember that most of the favourite hybrid teas may be obtained in climbing forms, including the in-my-opinion horridly coarse but ever-popular *Peace*.

Primulas

The vast family of primulas contains some of the loveliest and most reliable of plants, ranging from the pale primrose of our woods to the tall Asiatics and their hybrids, about which I propose to write today. Generally speaking, this class or group enjoys a moist soil and a shady place; and as there is a constant demand for plants that will thrive in shade, awkward to satisfy, the primulas will be found very useful as well as beautiful.

Of them all, I least like *Florindae*, the Tibetan cowslip, with its somewhat untidy drooping yellow bells, but it is a fool-proof plant of amazing vigour, setting so much seed that you could naturalize it anywhere by scattering it in handfuls or by transplating clumps of the innumerable seedlings. There are hybrid forms, mostly in rosy-brick red which I greatly prefer to the original type. *Primula japonica* and *Primula pulverulenta* are perhaps the most familiar to the amateur gardener; the Bartley strain of *pulverulenta*, downy, and softly coloured like a ripe peach, is one of my favourites, but I find it hard to choose between the Asthore hybrids, and *Bulleyana* orange-yellow, and *sikkimensis* pale-yellow, and *chionantha*, ivory-white as cream.

There are many others of the shade-loving moisture-loving primulas. Once you start on them, there seems to be no end. Don't we all know the mauve *denticulata*, and *capitata mooreana*, and the little low-growing *rosea* which will increase itself all over the place where it finds itself happy? What a wonderful and varied plant family this is, some of them coming from such remote regions as the high mountains of Central Asia, and one our own tiny native *farinosa*, the bird's-eye primrose, snuggling along the banks of the becks of our northern moors.

Narcissi

The great family of the Narcissi is surely one of the most dependable. Wheresoever you plant them, the bulbs never fail to throw up the flower already conceived inside them, going on year after year, increasing in quantity until they begin to deteriorate in quality, when you can dig them up and make two score when you once planted one. There is something very satisfactory in lifting a huge clump by spade from the turf, and dividing the children of those brown onions from their parents, to grow on into a new plump life of their own.

I called them narcissi, for there is really no difference between the daffodil and the narcissus. It is simply a distinction popularly made between Trumpet and Flat-face. This is putting it very crudely, but for practical purposes it will serve. Whichever sort you intend to plant, the sooner you do it the better. October is not too late, but September is better still. If you want exhibition blooms, you will plant them in bare beds; but if you want a drift looking right and happy, you will fling a handful over a stretch of grass and plant them where they fall and roll. Never mind if their distribution seems irregular as the bulbs lie waiting on top of the ground. It will look all right when they come up next March.

For my own part, I like to see them growing in groups of separate varieties, rather than mixed. There are now so many varieties that the choice becomes bewildering, also slight differences in price for which I must refer you to the catalogues. Here are a few trumpet daffodils that I would not be without: Golden Harvest, Magnificence, Rembrandt, all yellow, and in the cheaper yellows I remain faithful to King Alfred and Winter Gold, although I know the experts regard them as having been superseded. If you like the purity of white trumpets, you could not do better than Mount Hood; the more familiar white Beersheba, lovely though she is, tends to flop on her stalk and is preferable as a cut flower than naturalized in the garden. The old so-called pink daffodil, Mrs. R. O. Backhouse, is a slight favourite of mine.

Among the large-cupped narcissi, Fortune is still one of the best. I believe when it first appeared on the market it cost £500 a bulb. John Evelyn, ivory white, I have found to be a tremendous increaser, so very good for naturalizing though not much good for picking. Carlton is a fine and faithful golden-yellow. Aranjuez, with a yellow perianth widely edged in deep orange-red, suffers from nothing but its name at which the English are apt to make a bad shy shot sounding like Arran-juice. I must end this very short list with La Riante, well named, for it really does seem to laugh with all the gaiety of spring.

Miniature narcissi

I would like to refer to the tiniest of the narcissus family. I suppose I ought to start with the tiniest of all, *minimus*, a little yellow trumpet no more than 3 in. high, which likes peat but hates manure, and is perhaps seen at its best in a pan on the staging of a cold greenhouse, where it will not get splashed or dashed by February weather and can be appreciated at a convenient eye level. In fact, all the miniature narcissi make pretty pot plants if a few bulbs can be spared for that purpose, though all of them are hardy and can be grown out-of-doors, on a rockery, or in a trough, or naturalized in grass.

The very strongly scented ones gain by the more intimate position of a pan on the staging. The Pyrenean *juncifolius* certainly does, for the fragrance of its 6-in.-high bright yellow flowers, rising amongst rush-like leaves, would be wasted on the open air. *Juncifolius* is a treasure, and well worth one panful as a treat.

The *bulbocodium* or hoop-petticoat daffodil is an easy one, which you may have seen naturalized in grass almost by the acre at Wisley, and very pretty it is, small and tight-waisted, springing out into a crinoline. It does not like to be too dry: and the same may be said of *cyclamineus*, which lays its ears back as though frightened or in a tantrum, like the small cyclamens. *Narcissus triandrus albus*, called Angel's Tears, also lays its ears back. Ivory-white, about 6 in. high, most delicately pretty, it will grow in broken shade, where it looks like a little ghost, weeping.

Junipers

Some people nourish a prejudice against yews. They think them funereal. This is purely a question of association, because yews are often found in churchyards, but people have their prejudices, and it is no good arguing against them. 'A man convinced against his will, is of the same opinion still,' so if people don't like the dark yew in their garden let me suggest a substitute, the Irish juniper, *J. hibernica* or *fastigiata*, which possesses the same rigid columnar shape, equally valuable as the full-stop or exclamation mark I recommended for a focal point, but less severe and grim, being blue-green, almost glaucous, in colour, not that dark almost black-green that some people find so gloomy. Personally, I like all gloomy trees; perhaps I have a melancholy streak in my character; anyhow, I like the dark background they make, reminding me of cypresses in Italy and of stone-pines in Spain.

The junipers have many advantages. For one thing, they are lime-lovers, meaning that owners of gardens on an alkaline chalky soil can plant them with every hope of success. This does not imply that they will not grow elsewhere: I have seen a creeping juniper, a spreading type, growing in peaty soil in Scotland, ramping wild all over a woodland stretch under silver birches. I brought home an armful of its dead branches, and used them as smouldering pokers to push into a wood-fire on my hearth, waving them about the room as one would wave old stalks of lavender or rosemary, redolent as incense but far fresher and less heavy on the air. I took this to be *J. horizontalis*, apparently the only variety which does not favour a limestone soil, but on enquiry discovered that it was the common juniper, dwarfed by deer and rabbits eating it in the winter.

It made a beautiful, stiff, dark carpet under the pallor of the silver birches. Little burns dribbled, in a natural irrigation. Their bubbles rose like bursting pearls over the shallow pebbles. It made me wish to possess not a more-or-less-formal but a completely informal garden, with wild woodland on the margin. I don't mean to complain about my own garden. It serves me and satisfies me quite well, except at the moments when I get into despair over it; very frequent moments, when I long to have some other sort of garden, quite different; a garden in Spain, a garden in Italy, a garden in Provence, a garden in Scotland.

One can't have everything: and one mustn't be too greedy. Committed as I am to a more-or-less-formal garden, I would very strongly recommend the Irish juniper to anyone who wants a full-stop focal point where it seems necessary. It has an architectural value, of great importance in even the smallest acreage.

October

Strawberry grape

A new pleasure has abruptly entered my life, and I should like to pass it on to others: the Strawberry grape. It is perfectly hardy here in Kent, where an outdoor specimen, twenty years old, covers a cottage, and is now heavy with ruby-pink bunches this autumn even after the cruel winter of 1946–47. My own little vine is only in its second year, but is already fruiting so generously that a number of bunches had to be suppressed; it would have been unwise as well as unkind to let so young a thing carry more than eight. But I foresee that it will go on in strength and wealth.

The great point about this grape is its flavour. I hope the professional nurseryman will forgive me if I say that his claims for his wares sometimes read better on paper than they turn out in fact; his colours glow brighter, his fruit tastes sweeter, and the vigour of his plants is beyond belief. But the Strawberry grape really does taste of strawberries – the little Alpine or wood strawberry. One unkind guest said it tasted of peardrops, but I stick to my conviction.

Another vine which is giving me great pleasure at the moment is *Vitis heterophylla*, an East Asian. You can't eat it, but you can pick it and put it in a little glass on your table, where its curiously coloured berries and deeply cut leaves look oddly artificial, more like a spray designed by a jeweller out of dying turquoises than like a living thing. Yet it will grow as a living thing, very rapidly, on the walls of your house, or over a porch, hanging in lovely swags of its little blue berries, rather subtle, and probably not the thing that your next-door-neighbour will bother to grow or perhaps doesn't know about. There are some obvious plants which we all grow: useful things, and crude. We all know about them. But the real gardener arrives at the point when he wants something rather out of the common run; and that is why I make these suggestions which might turn your garden into something a little different and a little more interesting than the garden of the man next door.

Autumn colours

A note on some special small trees for autumn colour may not come amiss. *Crataegus crus-galli*, the Cockspur Thorn, turns as scarlet as you could wish in October, and is a tough little tree which will flourish anywhere; against the dark background of a hedge he will look splendid. *Disanthus cercidifolium* hangs itself with round leaves like golden coins. *Cornus Kousa* and *Cornus florida rubra*; *Berberis Thunbergii atropurpurea splendens*; *Parrotia persica*; *Prunus Sargentii*; all these will flame through October until the leaves come off. It is a good plan to plant them where at some moment of the day they will catch the sunlight; and it is more effective to plant two or three in a clump than some isolated specimen. This advice applies to most plants, but especially to those designed to make a bonfire of colour in the rich, mellow days of autumn.

Peach trees

Some friends of mine planted a small peach tree six years ago. They stuck it in and left it to make what it could of itself. This year they have picked over 900 peaches from it, fine large fruits, excellent for dessert, for jam or for bottling. We usually associate peaches with a sunny wall – and how warm the rosy fruit looks, hanging against old brick of much the same colour – but this tree stands out in the open, unsheltered, unprotected, and unpruned. The branches had to be propped, they were so heavy; but apart from a generous mulch of manure, that was all the attention it got. A good reward, I thought, for so little trouble.

Of course, if you could find a sheltered corner, say in the angle formed by two hedges, giving protection from cold winds, it might do even better; and there is no doubt that if you threw a veil of tiffany or butter-muslin or even some old lace curtains over the blossom when frost threatens in April or May, you would be doing much to safeguard the crop. This would apply especially in a hard winter and a draughty spring. My friends treated their tree rough: they let it take its chance, and it took it. So I thought I would advise other people to try the same experiment.

After all, what do you risk? A guinea to buy the tree. Then you wait for a year or two, and then you start to pick the fruit. You get a couple of dozen after three years. After six years you get 900 – not a bad investment. It would certainly succeed in the Home Counties and in the South, and I have heard of a regular orchard of peaches in Essex, though I should not like to venture an opinion about the North. But, given a reasonably mild district, there seems no reason why this experiment should not be turned into profit as well as pleasure. The importation of foreign fruit has not improved the English market, but the home grower can still sell peaches or nectarines for anything up to eightpence each, and 900 eightpences would make a useful contribution to the current expenses involved in keeping up a garden.

The peach my friends grow is called *Grosse Mignonne*, and that has proved its quality; but varieties specially recommended for this rather unorthodox method, i.e. not fan-trained against a wall, are *Peregrine*, *Sea Eagle*, and *Duke of York*.

I have mentioned nectarines. This most delicious fruit could, of course, be grown in the same way, as a bush in the open. *Early Rivers* and *Humboldt* are both good varieties.

Quinces

It always surprises me that we in this country should neglect to plant some of the fruits which are now seldom to be seen save as survivals in some old garden. For example, the common quince. In some parts of France you see it growing as a hedgerow plant, its great yellow pear-shaped fruits heavily hanging for any thrifty villager to pick and turn into jelly or quince-cheese. It grows in the hedgerows there as thick as blackberries in an English lane. Why don't we plant it in our gardens here, as our grandfathers did?

It is of the easiest possible cultivation, and will do in almost any type of soil, though naturally it will be happiest in a nice light loam with plenty of humus. It appreciates moisture, so long as it is not completely waterlogged. It requires no pruning or spraying. So far as I know, it suffers from no form of disease. It is self-fertile. Birds to not attack it, and the fruit ripens too late for the wasps. The blossom comes late, and thus seldom has to endure danger from frost. It lives to a great age and is a regular and reliable cropper. It makes all the difference to stewed apples or to an apple-pie. It can, and should, be turned as I have said into delicious jelly, marmalade, or cheese. If it is on its own roots, as it usually is, it can readily be increased from its own suckers.

To this catalogue of excellences, add that it is very beautiful, both in May when it flowers and in October when it ripens, and you will not wonder that I should demand a revival of planting the common quince.

So far as its beauty goes, I think there are two ideal situations to choose for it. One would be near water, so that the branches would hang over and be reflected in a pool, a stream, or even a pond. The other would be immediately beneath a bedroom window, so that in the spring you could look down into the wide upturned faces of the shell-pink blossom amongst the young leaves and the wiry tangle of very black twigs, and in the autumn on to the fat golden fruits. Only the occupant of the upper room could tell the delight of observing the quince throughout the cycle of the seasons.

Then, as a postscript, I might put in a good word for the bullace. This, like the quince, is a tree seldom seen except in old gardens. It is, I believe, the child of a marriage between a damson and a plum. It has no ornamental value, but crops inordinately every year, small purple fruits which bring a good marketing price if you have the patience and leisure to pick them, and can also be used to make bullace wine

The autumn garden

The autumn garden. . . . It has its beauty; especially, perhaps, a garden with an old orchard attached to it. When I was very small, about four years old, I suppose, a line of poetry entered into my consciousness, never to leave it again:

Rye pappels drop about my head.

I had no idea what rye pappels might be, but they held a magic, an enchantment for me, and when in later life I identified them as the ripe apples of Andrew Marvell's poem they had lost nothing of their enchantment in the process of growing up.

Coming home from abroad, after an interval when the season had time to change from late summer into autumn, it struck me how *pink* and green the autumn garden was. Not bronze and blue, the colours we associate with the turning woods and the hazy distance and the blue smoke of bonfires along the hedgerows. The woods had not turned yet, but in the orchard the apples were rosy and in the garden the leaves of the peonies were pink, and so were the leaves of the common azaleas, and so were the leaves of *Parrotia persica* and the leaves of that other little tree with the lovely name *Liquidambar*, and the leaves of *Prunus Sargentii*, so soon to drop, alas, from the row in which I had planted them along the top of a rosy-red brick retaining wall.

The naked, reddish stems of the Belladonna lily (*Amaryllis*) had shot up in that surprising way they have, and were opening their clusters of pink flowers. This is a bulbous plant well worth growing, for it is reasonably hardy in the open ground in a sunny, well-drained position, preferably at the foot of a wall, and it supplies flowers for picking at a time when choice-looking flowers are rare. What it likes is lots of water in the early summer, while it is making its leaves, and then it likes to be left alone while the leaves disappear and nothing is seen until the flowering stems shoot up all of a sudden on an October morning.

The Michaelmas daisies were also rioting pink in the garden. All the sorts called *Beechwood*, *Beechwood Charm*, *Beechwood Challenger*, and that specially good one called

Harrington's Pink. Some people tell me that *Harrington's Pink* is not a good doer. I can say only that it does very well here in ordinary conditions, and that I have no complaint to make against it. It thrives, adding its bit of brighter pink to the rich scale of colouring leaves in the incarnadine symphony of October.

Cobaea scandens and Rosa Nevada

October is the time for the garden to be taken to pieces and replanted if necessary for next year. It is also the month that ushers in the long dark evenings when one makes seed lists under the lamp, pure pleasure and no worry; no slugs, no rabbits, no moles, no frosts, no damping-off. An interesting and unusual plant which should find a place is *Cobaea scandens*, which sounds more attractive under its English name of cups-and-saucers. This is a climber, and an exceedingly rapid one, for it will scramble eight to ten feet high in the course of a single summer. Unfortunately it must be regarded as an annual in most parts of this country, and a half-hardy annual at that, for although it might be possible with some protection to coax it through a mild winter, it is far better to renew it every year from seed sown under glass in February or March. Pricked off into small pots in the same way as you would do for tomatoes, it can then be gradually hardened off and planted out towards the end of May. In the very mild counties it would probably survive as a perennial.

It likes a rich, light soil, plenty of water while it is growing, and a sunny aspect. The ideal place for it is a trellis nailed against a wall, or a position at the foot of a hedge, when people will be much puzzled as to what kind of a hedge this can be, bearing such curious short-stemmed flowers, like a Canterbury Bell with tendrils. Unlike the Canterbury Bell, however, the flowers amuse themselves by changing their colour. They start coming out as a creamy white; then they turn apple-green, then they develop a slight mauve blush, and end up a deep purple. A bowl of the mixture, in its three stages, is a pretty sight, and may be picked right up to the end of October.

If you are now thinking that a half-hardy annual such as *Cobaea scandens* is too much trouble, and perhaps want something more permanent than you can get out of a seed packet, do consider the rose called *Nevada*. It got an Award of Merit from the R.H.S. in 1949, and well it deserved it. This is not a climber, but a shrubby type, forming an arching bush up to seven or eight feet in height, smothered with great single white flowers with a centre of golden stamens. One of its parents was the Chinese species rose *Moyesii*, which created a sensation when it first appeared and has now become well known. For those who are interested in such pedigrees, the other parent was *La Giralda*, a cross between that grand old Hybrid Perpetual, *Frau Karl Druschki*, and *Mme Edouard Herriot*. The grievance against *Moyesii* is that it flowers only once, in June; but *Nevada*, unlike *Moyesii*, has the advantage of flowering at least twice during the summer, in June and again in August, with an extra trickle of odd flowers right into the autumn. One becomes confused among the multitude of roses, I know, but *Nevada* is really so magnificent that you cannot afford to overlook her. A snowstorm in summer, as her name implies. And so little bother. No pruning; no staking; no tying. And nearly as thornless as dear old *Zéphyrine Drouhin*. No scent, I am afraid; she is for the eye, not for the nose.

Plaintive letters reach me from time to time saying that if I do not like herbaceous borders what would I put in their place? It is quite true that I have no great love for herbaceous borders or for the plants that usually fill them – coarse things with no delicacy or quality about them. I think the only justification for such borders is that they shall be perfectly planned, both in regard to colour and to grouping; perfectly staked; and perfectly weeded. How many people have the time or the labour? The alternative is a border largely composed of flowering shrubs, including the big bush roses; but for those who still desire a mixed border it is possible to design one which will (more or less) look after itself once it has become established.

It could be carried out in various colour schemes. Here is an idea for one in red and purple and pink: Polyantha roses *Dusky Maiden*, *Frensham*, *Donald Prior*; musk roses *Wilhelm*, *Pink Prosperity*, *Cornelia*, *Felicia*, *Vanity*; the common old red herbaceous peonies, with Darwin tulips planted amongst them if you like; and a front edging of the dwarf asters and daisies such as *Dresden China* and *Rob Roy*, which makes big mats and go on for ever, and even violets for early flowering, and some patches of *Fragaria indica*, the ornamental strawberry with bright red fruits all through the summer. Nor would I despise a counterpane, at intervals, of *Cotoneaster horizontalis*, crawling over the ground with its herring-bone spine, its small box-like leaves of darkest green and its brilliantly red berries in autumn.

Another idea, pale and rather ghostly, a twilight-moonlight border. *Forsythia* along the back; musk roses *Danae*, *Moonlight* and *Thisbe* in the middle; evening primroses, *Oenothera biennis*, self-sowing; *Iris ochroleuca*, tall and white and yellow; creamy peonies; and a front carpet of silver-foliage artemisias and stachys.

Of course, these are only the roughest indications, outlines to be filled in. The main thing, it seems to me, is to have a foundation of large, tough, untroublesome plants with intervening spaces for the occupation of annuals, bulbs, or anything that takes your fancy. The initial outlay would seem extravagant, but at least it would not have to be repeated, and the effect would improve with every year.

More about Quinces

As this month and the next bring round the time for planting shrubs, the ornamental quinces should not be forgotten. They may take a little while to get going, but, once they have made a start, they are there for ever, increasing in size and luxuriance from year to year. They need little attention, and will grow almost anywhere, in sun or shade. Although they are usually seen trained against a wall, notably on old farmhouses and cottages, it is not necessary to give them this protection, for they will do equally well grown as loose bushes in the open or in a border, and, indeed, it seems to me that their beauty is enhanced by this liberty offered to their arching sprays. Their fruits, which in autumn are as handsome as their flowers, make excellent jelly; in fact, there is everything to be said in favour of this well-mannered easy-going, obliging and pleasantly old-fashionable plant.

The only grievance that people hold against it, for which the poor thing is scarcely to be blamed is its frequent change of name. It started its career as *Pyrus japonica*, and became familiarly known as Japonica, which simply means Japanese, and is thus as silly as calling a plant 'English' or 'French.' It then changed to Cydonia, meaning quince: *Cydonia japonica*, the Japanese quince. Now we are told to call it *Chaenomeles*, but as I don't know what that means, beyond a vague idea that *chae* means hairy and *meles* means sombre or black, and as, furthermore, I am not at all sure how to pronounce it, I think I shall stick to Cydonia, which is in itself a pretty word.

There are many varieties. There is the old red one, *C. lagenaria*, hard to surpass in richness of colour, beautiful against a grey wall or a whitewashed wall, horrible against modern red brick. There is *C. nivalis*, pure white, safely lovely against any background. There is *C. Moreloesii*, or the Apple-blossom quince, whose name is enough to suggest its shell-pink colouring. There is *Knaphill Scarlet*, not scarlet at all but coral-red; it goes on flowering at odd moments throughout the summer long after its true flowering season is done. There is *C. cathayensis*, with small flowers succeeded by the biggest green fruits you ever saw – a sight in themselves. Finally, if you want a prostrate kind, there is *C. Simonii*, spreading horizontally, with dark red flowers, much to be recommended for a bank or a rock-garden.

Autumn colouring

If you are thinking of planting for autumn colouring, this is the time to look at the flaming shrubs and trees and to make your choice. In spring and summer one tends to forget the autumn days, but, when they arrive, with their melancholy and the spiders' webs so delicately and geometrically looped from the hedges, how grateful we are for the torch of a little tree or the low smoulder of leaves on azaleas and peonies. I feel sure that these effects should be concentrated into one area of the garden, preferably at a distance if space allows, so that they may be seen from the windows in a rabble incarnadine.

A visit to a local nursery will supply many suggestions. For my own part, I would plant a backing of the Cockspur thorn, *Crataegus crus-galli*, and of the Scarlet Oak, *Quercus coccinea*, slow in growth but magnificently red in its October–November colour. If I had enough room, I would plant *Koelreuteria paniculata* behind these; it makes a tall tree in time; is seldom seen in our gardens; and contributes an astonishing pyramid of pink, yellow, and green at this time of the year. Then in front of all these I would plant *Prunus Sargentii*, a small tree pretty enough with its pink blossom in spring, but lovelier still in autumn when its leaves turn red, especially if you have planted it so that the early morning sun or the late afternoon sun can illuminate it and make the leaves transparent. This is a very important point, I think, which any gardener planting for autumn colour should observe: the transparency against the sun. I should then plant a whole host of autumn-colouring in front of these; little trees such as the peat-loving *Disanthus cercidifolius*, whose small round leaves dangle like golden coins; *Cornus Kousa*; *Acer griseum*, *Nandina domestica*; *Euonymus alatus*, a most brilliant pink; *Rhus continoides foliis-purpureis*, the American sumach; and the low-growing, rounded bush of *Berberis Thunbergii*. As a ground covering for the front, there is a charming little bristly rose called *nitida*, which creeps about and forms a mat of blackish-red leaf and stem, not very showy from afar off perhaps, but pretty and unusual close to.

There are only a very few of the suggestions that could be made. I have not even mentioned the ornamental vines, such as *Coignetiae*, or the larger trees such as *Cercidiphyllum* or *Parrotia persica*.

Sweet peas

A complaint commonly brought against many of the modern or 'improved' varieties of favourite old flowers is that they have lost their scent. In some cases this complaint is justified; in others not. The one which I want to consider in this article is the Sweet Pea, and it is quite an appropriate moment to do so, since this is the month when seeds may still be sown in pots for wintering in a frame and planting out next spring.

The true Sweet Pea, *Lathyrus odoratus*, small, hooded, and not remarkable for any beauty of colour, was originally sent from Italy in 1699 by a Father Cupani to Dr. Robert Uvedale, headmaster of the Grammar School at Enfield, Middlesex. Of Father Cupani I know nothing, but Dr. Uvedale, schoolmaster and horticulturist, seems to have been something of a character. He had a fine collection of foreign plants, which after his death in 1722 were sold to Sir Robert Walpole for his garden at Houghton in Norfolk. Of Dr. Uvedale it was said that 'his flowers were choice, his stock numerous, and his culture of them very methodical and curious.' Amongst them was the Sweet Pea, native of southern Italy and Sicily, and it is this which I should like to see restored to favour in this country.

Undoubtedly the Grandiflora and Spencer hybrids offer a greater range of colour, a greater solidity and length of stalk, and more flower-heads to a stalk, nor can it be said that they lack the fragrance which gives them their popular name. But compared with the fragrance of the humble little wild-ling they have nothing to boast about in that respect. It must be realized that the wild pea is not showy, in fact its pink and purple are very washy and the individual flowers are small, but they have a certain wistful delicacy of appearance and the scent of even half a dozen in a bunch is astonishing.

Of course it is no good attempting to grow them on the elaborate system of training one stem up a bean-pole and suppressing all side shoots; they must be left to scramble up twiggy pea-sticks in a tangle and kept entirely for picking, in an unwanted but sunny corner of the kitchen garden.

At the end of their season they can be left to set their own seed and a supply be thus ensured. I know for a fact that they do set and ripen their seed in this island, for I have seen them doing it in a private garden quite far north and came away, I am glad to say, with a generous handful which I hope to have growing in my own garden next summer.

A native iris

A spike of the brightest orange caught my eye, half hidden by a clump of *Berberis Thunbergii* which had turned very much the same colour. They were both of an extraordinary brilliance in the low afternoon sunshine. I could not remember if I had planted them deliberately in juxtaposition, or if they had come together by a fortunate chance. Investigation revealed further spikes: three-sided seed-pots cracked wide open to expose the violet clusters of the berries within.

This was our native *Iris foetidissima* in its autumn dress, our only other native iris being the yellow waterside flag, *I. pseudo-acorus*. No one would plant *I. foetidissima* for the sake of its name, which in English is rendered the Stinking iris and derives from the unpleasant smell of the leaves if you bruise them. There is, however, no need to bruise leaves, a wanton pastime, and you can call it the Gladdon or Gladwyn iris if you prefer, or even the Roast-beef Plant. Some etymologists think that Gladdon or Gladwin are corruptions of Gladiolus, owing to a similarity between the sword-like leaves; but I wish someone would tell me how it got its roast-beef name.

Its flowers, small and of a dingy mauve, are of no value or charm, nor should we be wise to pick them, because it is for the seed-pods that we cherish it. Not that it needs much cherishing, and is even one of those amiable plants that will tolerate shade. Strugglers with shady gardens, or with difficult shaded areas, will doubtless note this point. The seed-pods are for late autumn and winter decoration indoors, for the seeds have the unusual property of not dropping out when the pods bursts open, and will last for a long time in a vase; they look fine, and warm, under a table-lamp on a bleak evening. Miss Gertrude Jekyll used to advise hanging the bunch upside down for a bit, to stiffen the stalks; I dare say she was right; she was usually right, and had an experimental mind.

Let me not claim for the Gladdon iris that its crop of orange berries makes a subtle bunch or one which would appeal to flower-lovers of very delicate taste; it is frankly as coarse as it is showy, and has all the appearance of having been brought in by a pleased child after an afternoon's ramble through the copse. Nevertheless, its brightness is welcome, and its coarseness can be lightened by a few sprays of its companion the berberis.

Careful cultivation

The more I see of finely-cared-for gardens, the more do I realize the high importance given to cultivation. The size of the garden has nothing to do with it: twenty acres or one acre or half an acre, it is all the same, so long as the love and knowledge are there.

Most of us amateur gardeners are inclined to stick in a

plant all anyhow, and leave it to take its chance, a chance which probably results in death to it and disappointment to us. Good gardeners, the gardeners who know their job, take far more trouble. They prepare the soil first, making it suitable for the plant they wish to put in; and then later on they look after it, caring for it in times of drought, cosseting it along for the first months of its young life, nourishing it in its middle-age, and never neglecting it even when it attains a ripe maturity.

I note, for example, that lawn-mowings are not wasted. They are spread in a thin mulch over beds. This, because if you heap them too thickly, they heat; therefore, never spread them more than two or three inches deep. The virtue of lawn-mowings is threefold: they keep weeds away, they retain moisture, and they supply humus to the soil as the green stuff rots down and returns its vegetable value into the ground it grew from. There is practically no plant in the garden that will not benefit from this mulching – flowering shrubs and flowering trees; herbaceous plants in the border; roses; anything and everything. Lilies are an exception.

Any top-dressing in the autumn is of benefit. Leaf-mould and compost ... I know that compost is a controversial point. No one, in theory, denies its value; but many people still say that it demands too much trouble and too much labour and time. It should be composed of the right ingredients and scientifically constructed in layers like an enormous sandwich; it requires turning and watering and aerating; but as most books on horticulture include instructions, notably on the well-known Indore method, I need not repeat the details here.

Failing compost or leaf-mould, a top dressing of bone-meal or hoof and horn in autumn in much to be recommended.

188

A few handfuls are easy to scatter, and supply a true, slow-acting food rather than a stimulant. Violent stimulants are apt to be dangerous, promoting a soft, quick growth when what the plant needs is a building-up of its underground constitution, to take effect not immediately and dramatically, but in months to come.

The principle, is always the same: you cannot expect your soil and your plants to go on giving you of their best if you are not prepared to give something back in return. This is as true of gardens as of human relationships.

A small greenhouse

There is no more amusing toy for the amateur gardener than a small greenhouse. It need not necessarily be heated, if he can be satisfied with plants that do not dread the frosts of winter but whose fragile petals suffer from the onslaught of heavy rain or hail. Such plants are better grown under the covering of glass, that transparent canopy which admits the light and excludes the unkindly deluge descending from overhead.

Surely many owners of such small greenhouses have turned them into a sort of Alpine house by now, filled with pans of winter-flowering bulbs such as the little crocuses, and early irises. There are so many, so easily grown, and so delightful to watch during the dark days. To go into the greenhouse and to see these little exquisite things in full flower on the staging in mid-winter takes us in a great stride towards the longed-for spring and bluffs us into believing that the cold dead months are behind us.

The squat pans stuffed with such treasures should be filled now without delay. Do not make the mistake I made last year of putting in the crocuses too sparsely. I thought they would look nicer if they had more room to develop, but I was wrong. They need to be crammed tight, as tight as can be, bulb touching bulb, like people squeezed together in a crowd. (I am referring, of course, to the species crocus and their hybrids, not to the ordinary garden variety.) The little irises, on the other hand, the *reticulata* irises for instance, gain by being given enough space to expand their lovely heads in liberty. Their bulbs should not be set nearer than a couple of inches apart.

These are the obvious things to grow for winter pleasure, but might I recommend something which will give pleasure under glass in May? We have such a foison of flowers out of doors in May that perhaps we do not want to be bothered with a pot plant just then. Still, I hope you will try it. It is an orchid called *Pleione Pricei*. Orchids sound difficult and expensive and far beyond our reach, but this one is easy and very pleasing to those who have eyes to see. It can be grown in the open, in a pocket of the rock-garden, for it is perfectly hardy, but then it suffers injury from the weather beating down on it, spoiling the flower just as it comes towards its consummation, so on the whole it is wiser to grow it in a pot or pan. It comes from Formosa; it likes a mixture of leaf-mould, sand, loam, and peat; and it must never be allowed to get dry.

Bringing plants indoors

The time has come to bring the tender pot-plants under cover for the winter. What a lot of pleasure they have given, throughout the summer months, those pots of the scented ivy-leaf pelargonium, those pots of the lemon-scented verbena, standing about in a casual way round our front doors or in odd corners of the garden, where you can tweak a leaf off and put it in your pocket or your buttonhole each morning. I wonder why people don't use pot-plants more frequently in this country, especially those people who have not a large garden and want to make use of every yard of space, easy to set a pot down on, taking up little room and giving little trouble apart from watering when the pots threaten to get dry.

Cottage people and people living in rural villages always seem so clever and so green-fingered about this sort of thing. They keep plants on their window-sills, flourishing for years, without any light or any attention at all, or so it seems. We might all usefully take a tip from the cottagers, and grow more pot-plants to set out of doors during the summer months and to bring indoors as soon as frost threatens, and then just to set them down on a window-sill in a room warmed by an ordinary fire, enough to keep the frost out.

This is also a suitable time to take cuttings of any favourite shrub to keep up the supply. There is something immensely satisfactory about a nursery of little rooted plants, growing along, waiting to be planted out or given away. They strike most easily in small pots or in a propagating frame, which need be nothing more elaborate than a shallow wooden box with some sheets of glass or a handlight placed over it until the roots have had time to form. You can save yourselves trouble by getting the prepared John Innes Compost for cuttings, supplied by any nurseryman or seedsman, or you can make it for yourselves out of one part loam, two parts peat, and one part sand. This is especially useful for cuttings to be raised under glass, but you will find that many cuttings will root out of doors, if you set them *very firmly* (this is important) in a shallow trench made by one slice of the spade and filled in with coarse sharp sand. You must not expect every single one of them to respond to this rougher method, but even if you get only twenty-five out of a hundred it is still very much worth while.

And by the way, a bottle of hormone preparation, such as Seradix A, will go a long way towards helping your cuttings to strike the desirable roots.

Two long-flowering shrubs

Two shrubs with an amazingly long flowering period are *Colutea arborescens* and *Colutea media*, the Bladder Sennas. They have been flowering profusely for most of the summer, and were still very decorative in the middle of October. Of the two I prefer the latter. *C. arborescens* has yellow flowers; but although *media* is perhaps the more showy they go very prettily together, seeming to complement one another in their different colouring. Graceful of growth with their long sprays of acacia-like foliage, amusingly hung with the bladders of seed-pods which give them their English name, the bright small flowers suggest swarms of winged insects. They are the easiest possible cultivation, doing best in a sunny place, and having a particular value in that they be used to clothe a dry bank where few other things would thrive, nor do they object to an impoverished stony soil. They are easy to propagate, either by cuttings or by seed, and they may be kept shapely by pruning in February, within a couple of inches of the old wood.

There is also *Colutea orientalis*, which I confess I have never seen. This has the same coppery flowers as *C. media*, itself a hybrid of *arborescens* and *orientalis*, but is said to be less generous of its flowers and to depend for its charm chiefly on the grey or glaucous quality of its leaf. One might try them all three, especially in a rough place. I know that highbrow gardeners do not consider them as very choice. Does that matter? To my mind they are delicately elegant, and anything which will keep on blooming right into mid-October has my gratitude.

By the way, they are *not* the kind of which you can make senna-tea. Children may thus regard them without suspicion and will need little encouragement to pop the seed-pods. It is as satisfactory as popping fuchsias.

Hedges

Hedges appear to worry a lot of people, so let me revert to the subject at this hedge-planting time of year. Hedges can be divided roughly into two sorts: those which flower and those which do not.

Hedges which do not flower are mostly well known. Yew is without question my own favourite, and is not nearly so slow-growing as most people imagine, but it has two drawbacks: it is poisonous to cattle, so you cannot plant it where your own or other people's cows are likely to browse on it; and it is expensive, so you cannot plant it unless your purse is deep. Privet I cannot abide, but it is the cheapest of all, even cheaper than *Lonicera nitida*, and I suppose that people wanting a solid, almost indestructible barrier will always continue to plant it. *Lonicera nitida* became the rage for hedging some years ago, and there is much to be said in its favour, especially if you are prepared to clip it two or three times a year to keep it neat and tidy. *Cupressus macrocarpa* also became the rage for hedging some years ago, but it has not stood the test of inland frosts. I would not advise anyone to plant a hedge of *C. macrocarpa* unless living near the sea or in an area free from hard frost.

Beech makes a magnificent hedge in time, especially if it can be allowed to grow really tall, 20 ft. high or so. It has the pleasing habit of retaining its fox-brown leaves through the winter until they get pushed off by the bright green young leaf of spring. Hornbeam has the same habit and is of faster growth than beech; also it is better suited to the heavier soils, but it is more twiggy and somehow lacks the dense nobility of beech; a good, useful hedge none the less. Holly has many merits, but is slow in growth and expensive to buy. The myrobolan, or cherry plum, is quick growing, strong, and relatively cheap, and may be used in a mixed hedge, for one must not forget the charm and interest of a well-chosen mixture.

I have left the thorns to the last. Perhaps they should come under the heading of flowering hedges, since they will flower if not chopped too closely. The hawthorn or quick makes probably the toughest, cheapest hedge for boundaries, although one might not elect to put it in the heart of the garden. Usually regarded as a farm-hedge, it is perhaps too ordinary for mention here; if so, I must apologize for making the reminder.

Another look at shapes

At this time of year there are plants to be scrapped. I feel sure that one of the secrets of good gardening is always to remove, ruthlessly, any plant one doesn't like. Heart-breaking though it may be to chop down a tree one planted years ago, it is the right thing to do if that tree is now getting in the way and keeping the sun off something else that needs it. And so with everything: scrap what does not satisfy and re-place it by something that will.

I feel sure also that the autumn is the time to look closely at the shapes and forms of shrubs and trees in their setting. Even in the smallest garden there is probably some branch that would be better lopped off, some shrub that would look better with some discipline and control. Shape, in a garden, is so important, if we regard, as I think we should, gardening as an extension of architecture; in other words the, garden as an outdoor extension of the house.

Gardening is endlessly experimental, and that is the fun of it. You go on trying and trying, testing and testing, and sometimes you have failures but sometimes you have successes which more than make up for the failures.

Things in trees

We do not make nearly enough use of the upper storeys. The ground floor is just the ground, the good flat earth we cram with all the plants we want to grow. We also grow some climbers, which reach to the first-floor windows, and we may grow some other climbers over a pergola, but our inventiveness usually stops short at that. What we tend to forget is that nature provides some far higher reaches into which we can shoot long festoons whose beauty gains from the transparency of dangling in mid-air.

What I mean, briefly, is things in trees. For example, ivy. I am no great lover of the adhesive ivy glueing itself to walls in a dark, dowdy, dusty mass and mess full of old birds'-nests which ought to be cleared out. As Milton rightly remarked, ivy is never sere. Sometimes one wishes it were. One gets so bored by its persistent stuffy evergreen. I would suggest growing one of the variegated ivies up into a tree instead, where its white-and-green or gold-and-green can hang loosely from the branches, becoming almost diaphanous with the light around it. I know I shall be told that ivy strangles trees, and I may also be told that only a giraffe would notice anything unusual; still, I proffer the advice.

There is no need to stick to ivy. The gadding vine will do as well. The enormous shield-shaped leaves of *Vitis coignetiae*, turning a deep pink in autumn, amaze us with their rich cornelian in the upper air, exquisitely veined and rosy as the pricked ears of an Alsatian dog. Then, if you prefer June-July colour to October colour, there is that curious vigorous climber, *Actinidia Kolomikta*, which starts off with a wholly green leaf, then develops white streaks and a pink tip, and puzzles people who mistake its colouring habits for some new form of disease. Cats like it: and so do I, although I don't like cats.

I suggest to anybody who has got a rough hedge, say of thorn or privet, or any old hedge that he cannot afford to grub, but would like to clothe with something pleasing and unusual, to grow through it and across it during the summer, why not grow the hop? Some hop-plants appeared accidentally in just such a hedge bordering my garden, and I accepted them with delight. I should never have thought of planting them deliberately; they came of their own accord; and how grateful I have been to them ever since.

Let me enumerate their virtues.

(1) They grow as fast as any annual climber, such as Morning Glory or *Cobaea scandens*.

(2) Unlike those two, they are not annual but perennial, and will duly shoot up again year after year.

(3) They can be used as a quick climber over a pergola, to fill up gaps while you wait for your better climbers to mature; in fact, I can imagine a pergola clothed in nothing but hops, and very pretty it might be. The leaf is of a fine

design, and when the flower comes later it has all the dangling though far less ponderous beauty of a bunch of muscat grapes.

(4) You can make hop-pillows, stuffed with the dried flowers, very helpful to sufferers from insomnia.

(5) Finally, though perhaps I ought to have put this first in seasonal succession, you can pick young hop-shoots in March or April and use them as a vegetable. There is no waste in so doing, because every hop-hill will throw up far more shoots than it can carry, and the superfluous shoots have to be pruned away. The waste occurs only because few English house-wives or cooks realize that here they have a free supply of something that has a taste closely resembling fresh asparagus.*

Soil-exhaustion

I wonder whether other amateur gardeners suffer the same grief and rage as I, on discovering that a certain plant which one has thought secure for years in its established place suddenly sickens, peters out, and dies? There must be some scientific reason, and I wish I knew it. I suspect in my fumbling ill-informed way, that it has something to do with soil-exhaustion, meaning that a plant takes from the soil the nutriment it needs, and then won't thrive any longer after it has taken it. It is a well-known fact that the soil in which primulas have been grown for too long may become affected by what is called primula sickness; and this may well be the reason why other plants refuse to go on living and thriving in the same place year after year.

* A warning footnote. Hop-roots, properly called hop-hills, cannot be bought from any nurseryman. They have to be obtained from a local farmer or hop grower.

If I may quote examples from my own garden. I had, until last year a stretch of Sweet Woodruff bordering a paved path under Kent cobnuts. Sweet Woodruff being one of our native woodland plants, I imagined that it would go on happily for ever in the suitable conditions I had provided for it. Not so. It became black and spindly, and to all intent and purpose ceased to exist. I tried topping it up with some rich compost. No good at all. Compost was not what it craved for. But what did it crave for? How often one wishes that plants could speak, and how alarmed one would be if they did, much as Balaam must have been alarmed by his ass; however, I suppose one would get used to it; and how helpful it might be. 'Please could you supply me with some magnesium? I am deficient in chlorophyll, and my leaves are turning yellow. A few handfuls of magnesium would bring me round. A dose of Epsom salts might help. You haven't paid nearly enough attention to the trace-elements in my soil, and it is high time you did so.'

Another example from my own garden. For years past I have been growing polyanthus and coloured primroses under the same cob-nut trees. They used to be, if I may say so, a grand sight all through April and the first half of May. People came from far and wide to admire them. Last spring I noticed to my dismay that they were not as good and thick on the ground as usual. Even the seedlings I put out to fill up the gaps didn't thrive. Soil-exhaustion, I suppose; but what am I to do about it? I can't dig them all up and replant them somewhere else. Yet that is what they seem to demand. The Sweet Woodruff that has sown itself in other parts of the garden where I don't want it, looks as green and healthy as the original plants.

It all seems to suggest that the ancient theory of rotation

of crops may apply also to the pretty flowers we grow for our pleasure.

Chance seedlings

My esteemed colleague, ex-nurseryman, and bold plant-collector, Mr. Clarence Elliott, renowned throughout the gardening world, apparently has an aversion to weeding. Not to weeding delicately and tactfully done by himself, but to the ruthless and indiscriminate extermination of all vegetation unrecognizable in its infant stage to the jobbing or indeed the professional employee. Groundsel and chickweed, or seedlings of some precious primula, out they all come at the scrape of the hoe, and off they all go on to the rubbish heap together. This, as Mr. Elliott rightly remarks, effectively forfends desirable survivals. He has nothing good to say for so thorough a use of the hoe; he would prefer hand-weeding with his favourite tool, the widger. I sometimes find myself bitterly in agreement with him. But one cannot hand-widge over more than a given area: time does not allow, so what is to be done about it?

One answer to the question is to go round the garden oneself, putting a little stick beside any self-sown plant specially to be preserved.

I will give a practical example. That very ordinary but to my mind very beautiful *Cotoneaster horizontalis* sows itself all over the place, and chooses the oddest corner to sow itself in. Little dark-green herring-bone plants crop up everywhere, and seem to possess a special taste for putting themselves just where they will look best, but where we should never have dreamed of deliberately setting them. Such a small seedling appeared once at the right angle formed by a yew-hedge, and I let it grow, and now it makes a great fan

of green and scarlet at the foot of the yew, a most unorthodox idea, abhorrent to any tidy-minded, hoe-wielding
gardener, as Mr. Elliott would say, but oh, how dear to me!

It is something to have saved seedlings like this from
destruction. I saved a lot more *Cotoneaster horizontalis*,
'rubbishy little things, only fit to be thrown away', and
planted them out on a sloping bank between azaleas. They
have taken two or three years to make any show, but now
they are fanning out and beginning to look fine under the
flaming red foliage of the azaleas. On a wall opposite climbs
a vine with huge red leaves, and above that a row of Sar-
gent's cherry turns pink; it is all very ruddy and florid.

Incidentally, the cotoneaster is much to be commended
as a ground cover for the discouragement of weeds, and, if
you don't want a lot of wasps' nests in your garden, is a
sumptuous collecting-ground for queen wasps when it
comes into flower in May.

November

A shrub for August

A small shrub which I should like particularly to recommend is *Caryopteris clandonensis*. It flowers from August onwards, bright blue and fringed, at a time when flowering shrubs are rare. Prune it, not very hard, at the end of February, and it will make a rounded bush from three to four feet high. If you cannot obtain the variety *clandonensis*, the sorts named *Mastacanthus* or *tangutica* will do as well. They like a sunny place but are not fussy as to soil; and in order to obtain the best effect I should plant at least three in a clump.

Flowers for a mild climate

From the gardening point of view, those who live in the south of our island have certain undeniable advantages over those that live in the north. The climate is softer; a fact which undoubtedly influences those plants marked by an ominous little asterisk in nurserymen's catalogues, meaning 'Suitable only for mild localities.' Nevertheless, those who live in the north need not despair; indeed, there are times when they may exult, for there are some things they can grow to greater perfection. What about *Tropaeolum speciosum*, the flame nasturtium, with brilliant red trumpets among the small dark leaves? This is the glory of Scottish gardens, defeating most efforts to grow it in the south, even on the cool north side of a hedge. And what about the autumn gentian, *sino-ornata*, which will do also in the south, in a lime-free bed of almost pure leaf-mould, but which is even better in the cooler conditions of the north? There are few lovelier plants for the shortening days of autumn; low, brilliant trumpets of the purest blue, increasing rapidly into large clumps that can be pulled to pieces and replanted or given away. The coloured primroses and polyantha also seem to favour a cool climate; indeed, many of the old-fashioned double primroses have now become so rare as to be obtainable only from a few Scottish nurseries.

The *tropaeolum*, the gentian, and the primrose are plants for every purse; but where a few extra shillings can be afforded they might well be expended on the magnificent Himalayan lily, *Lilium giganteum*. Grown in light woodland, they are seen at their best. Eight to ten feet tall, they lift their spires heavily hung with white trumpets, and as heavily spiced with scent. One of these spires, cut and put in a room, scents the air almost too strongly for the average person to endure.

They are expensive to buy, but they are more economical than they sound. For one thing, you may buy younger bulbs at a much cheaper rate, and grow them on for yourself; and for another thing, a full-grown bulb (which dies after its first flowering) will give you a whole cluster of little bulbs round it, which you can plant out in a nursery-bed and thus, in three years' time, obtain ten or twelve for a fine group. Dig it up in October or November, to divide and replant. After this, you need never be without them. They like semishade; a rich mixture of leaf-mould and loam; manure if you can supply it, buried deep enough for their roots to reach; and a little bracken or other litter thrown over them to protect their tips against spring frost.

The medlar

The medlar is not a fruit I care much about; by the time it is ready to eat, it bears far too close a resemblance to a rotting or 'bletted' pear. It can, however, be made into a preserve, and the little tree certainly has a definite garden value, for in a favourable autumn the leaves turn into a motley of very beautiful variegated colours – pink, yellow, green, and brown, freckled with the russet fruits which always remind me of those knobbly objects you see attached to leather thongs on the flail-like hand-weapons of medieval warfare.

But although I may have no great affection for the medlar as a fruit, my affection for the cherry-plum or *Myrobolan* knows no bounds. I wish it could be planted more widely. It has every virtue. It grows quickly; it is pretty in the spring, with its white blossom; it reaches its supreme beauty when its fruit ripens in mid-summer and its branches droop with the weight of fruit almost to the ground. The branches then seem loaded with fat jewels of amber and topaz, like a tree in an oriental fairy-tale.

It crops generously, most years. Its fruit makes delicious jam, especially if you put in the kernels of the stones, when you get a sharp almond flavour, reminding you of kernels left in apricot jam. It also makes a good hedge. It is, I feel sure, a tree to plant both for your immediate pleasure and for the pleasure of your children after you.

Plant the gages, too. The old greengage and all the other gages, the *Cambridge*, the *Early Rivers*, the *Transparent*. This (November) is the time to order and plant them.

The 'worst' months

It is not easy to find flowers for this time of year. November and December are the worst months. One has to fall back upon the berried plants, and amongst these I think *Cotoneaster rugosa Henryi* is one of the best. It is a graceful grower, throwing out long, red-berried sprays, with dark green pointed, leathery leaves of especial beauty. It is not fussy as to soil and will flourish either in sun or shade, in fact, it can even be trained against a north wall, which is always one of the most difficult sites to find plants for in any garden. *Berberis Thunbergii*, either the dwarf form or the variety called *purpurea*, both so well known that perhaps they need no recommendation, will also thrive in sun or shade, and at this time of year flame into the sanguine colours of autumn. They should be planted in clumps in some neglected corner, and be left to take care of themselves until the time comes to cut them for what professional florists call 'indoor decoration,' but what you and I call, more simply, something to fill the flower vases with. They have the additional merit of lasting a very long time in water.

The leaves of the rugosa rose, *Blanc de Coubert*, in either the single or the double form, also turn a very beautiful yellow at this time of year and are good for picking. This rose has every virtue; the flowers are intensely sweet-scented, they persist all through the summer, they are succeeded by bright red hips in autumn, as round as little apples, and the whole bush is a blaze of gold in November. The only disadvantage, for a small garden, might be the amount of room the bush takes up; it is a strong grower, like most of the rugosas: and will eventually spread to a width of four or five feet and to a height of a tall man. It is, however, very shapely, with its rounded head, and it never straggles.

Planting cracks in paving

A correspondent makes the helpful suggestion that I might suggest how to fill up the cracks and spaces in stone paving. I take it that she means either crazy paving or square stone paving, or paving made from slabs of cement, poured in on the spot between a framework of wooden slats and left to 'set' with some wrinkled sacking laid over them to roughen the surface. This is a very economical home-made method; it also enables you to vary the size and shape of the slabs; and, especially if you incorporate into the wet cement some small pebbles known as 'beach' by builders, is almost indistinguishable from real stone once it has weathered.

I must assume, however, that my correspondent's paving is already laid, and is just waiting, stark and bare, to be planted with something that will take away the bareness. The first essential is that it shall be something which does not mind being walked upon. There was once a play called *Boots and Doormats*, which divided people into two categories: those who liked to trample and those who enjoy being trampled. Many big boots will walk down a paved path, and there are some meek doormats prepared to put up with such gruff treatment. The creeping thymes really enjoy being walked on, and will crawl and crawl, spreading gradually into rivulets and pools of green, like water slowly trickling, increasing in volume as it goes, until they have filled up all the cracks and crevices. The thymes are the true standby for anybody who wants to carpet a paved path.

There are others also. *Pennyroyal* does not mind what you do with it, and will give out its minty scent all the better for being bruised underfoot. *Cotula squalida* is much nicer than its name; it has tiny fern-like leaves, cowering very close down; no flower, but very resistant to hard wear and very easy to grow. All the *Acaenas* are useful; *Acaena Buchananii*, a silver-green, or *Acaena microphylla*, bronze in colour. A pity that such tiny things should have such formidable names, but they are neither difficult to obtain nor to establish.

Writing about crawly plants makes me think how prettily this notion could be extended in a rather original way. I imagine a level plot of ground, the size and shape of which would naturally depend upon the space available; I would hope only that it need not be *too* small. It could be square, round, oval, or rectangular. It should not be under the drip of trees, but part of it could be in the shade, for the shade-loving plants, and part in the sun for the sun-lovers. I imagine the whole of this plot well dug in preparation, with a couple of inches deep of sharp sand spread on top of the soil to keep away the weeds, or at any rate to facilitate their removal. Then you lay your stones, or your home-made cement slabs as I suggested. Of course, real stone is the gardener's ideal, but it is expensive, working out at about ten shillings a square yard, which is more than most of us can afford.

It will not matter much what you make your paving of, for it will soon get covered up with plants and will not show through. I imagine that you will keep the middle of this paved plot for walking on, and that you will there plant the plants that do not object to being trodden underfoot and crushed – the thymes, and the small mints, and the other things I recommended. But in this new imaginary garden-plot you will have scope to plant all sorts of things round the edges where they are in no danger of being walked on.

I imagine lumps of Thrift, green cushions of the particularly pleasing sort called *Armeria Corsica*, or the variety called *Vindictive*; I imagine also clumps of the low-growing daisy, *Bellis Dresden China*, as pink and pretty as its name suggests; and sun-roses (*Helianthemum*) foaming in all the delicate colours of terra-cotta, buff, yellow, and rose; and the little trailing *Gypsophila fratensis*, a cloud of minute shell-pink blossoms; and some mounds of saxifrage, interplanted with the tiny iris-like *Sisyrinchium angustifolium*, sometimes called Blue-eyed Grass, which sows itself everywhere; and I should have also some tufts of the small iris *pumila*, in blue or violet, and a plant or two of the shrubbery little *Aethionema warleyensis*.

The small bulbs would also find a place – the bright blue scillas, the darker grape-hyacinths, chionodoxa or Glory of the Snow, the miniature narcissi, crocuses both spring and autumn flowering. All of them love the cool root-run they find between stones. There is no end to the choice, and no reason why you should not achieve colour and interest throughout the seasons. The main thing to remember is that what you are really trying to do is to make a rock garden on the flat.

Sages

The family of the Sages is well known both in the kitchen-garden and the flower-garden. Some are aromatic herbs, scenting the hillsides in the sun of Mediterranean countries, and are associated in our minds with rough paths, goats and olives. The sage is altogether an amiable plant; indeed, its Latin name, *Salvia*, comes from *salvere*, to save, or heal, and one of its nicknames is *S. salvatrix*, which sounds very reassuring. The common clary, or *S. sclarea*, is also known as Clear Eye and See Bright, not to be confused with Eyebright, that tiny annual whose proper name is Euphrasia.

The French bestow a very genial personality on clary by calling it simply Toute Bonne, which to me at any rate suggests a rosy old countrywoman in a blue apron.

The kitchen sages make decorative clumps, for they can be had with reddish or variegated leaves as well as the ordinary grey-green. The garden sages are useful for the herbaceous border. I do not mean that half-hardy bedding-out plant beloved of the makers of public gardens, *S. splendens*, which should be forbidden by law to all but the most skilful handlers. I mean such old favourites as *S. virgata nemorosa*, a three-foot-high bushy grower whose blue-lipped flowers cluster amongst red-violet bracts and have the advantage of lasting a very long time in mid-summer; or *S. Grahamii*, equally familiar, with durable red flowers, a Mexican, reasonably but not absolutely hardy. A more recent introduction, not yet so well known as it should be, is *S. haematodes*, greatly to be recommended; it grows about five feet high in a cloud of pale blue rising very happily behind any grey-foliaged plant such as the old English lavender. This salvia grows readily from seed, especially if sown as soon as it ripens, and will in fact produce dozens of seedlings of its own accord. It is good for picking, if you bruise the stems or dip their tips for a few moments into boiling water.

Anybody with the time to spare should grow *S. patens*. It is a nuisance in the same way as a dahlia is a nuisance, because its tubers have to be lifted in autumn, stored in a frost-proof place, started into growth under glass in April, and planted out again at the end of May. The reason for this is not so much the tenderness of the tubers themselves as the risk that a late frost will destroy the young shoots; possibly the use of a cloche or hand-light might obviate this danger.

The amazing azure of the flowers, however, compensates for any extra trouble. Like the gentians, they rival the luminosity of the blue bits in a stained-glass window.

Tattery trees

Perhaps few people share my taste for tattered-bark trees. I must concede that it is a special taste. I must concede also that unless you have a fairly large garden you cannot afford the space even for one or two specimens set aside in a neglected corner, to grow taller and taller as the years go on. So this must be an article for the few, not for the many.

I like the tattery trees, whose bark curls off in strips like shavings. There is one called *Arbutus Menziesii*: with cinnamon-red bark which starts to peel of its own accord, and which you can then smooth away with your hand into something like the touch of sand-papered wood of a curious olive-green colour. It likes a sheltered corner, for it is not absolutely hardy. Then there is *Acer griseum*, the Paperbark maple, with mahogany-coloured bark replaced by a brighter orange underneath, and brilliantly red leaves in autumn. It is, in fact, one of the best for October–November colour. *Betula albo-sinensis* var. *septentrionalis* is a birch with a beautiful white-and-grey trunk. It is, I think, one of the loveliest, though *Betula japonica* drips with most attractive little catkins in spring.

Prunus serrula, sometimes sold as *serrula tibetica*, is a very striking tree with a shiny mahogany bark. This does not take on so shaggy an appearance as some, but sheds its outer covering in circular strips, leaving the trunk with annular ridges that make it look as though it were wearing bracelets. Reddish and glossy, the freshly-revealed surface suggests the French polish sometimes used on fine old tables. It should be grown in very rich soil and planted where it can be seen, with the sun shining on it.

Preparing beds for planting

One lesson that I have learnt is to plant things well from the start. A good start in life is as important to plants as it is to children: they must develop strong roots in a congenial soil, otherwise they will never make the growth that will serve them richly according to their needs in their adult life. It is important, it is indeed vital, to give a good start to any plant that you are now adding to your garden in this great planting month.

You may be planting some extra roses in this month of November, when roses are usually planted. Let me urge you to plant them with some peat and a handful of bone-meal mixed in with the peat. I did this last autumn on the re-commendation of some rose-grower, I think it may have been Mr. Wheatcroft, and the effect on the root growth of my experimental rose bushes was truly surprising to me when I dug them up this autumn to move them to another place. They had made a system of fibrous root such as I had never seen in so short a time. The reason is probably that peat retains moisture at the same time as giving good drainage, and that the bone-meal supplies nourishment.

It is usually supposed that roses enjoy a clay soil, and this I do believe to be true, having gardened in my early years on the stickiest clay to be found in the Weald of Kent. But what I now also believe to be true, is that although some plants such as roses will put up with a most disagreeable soil, they prefer to be treated in a more kindly fashion, having their bed prepared for them, dug out, and filled in with the type of soil they particularly favour. It is no use trying to grow the peat-lovers in an alkaline or chalky soil; everybody knows that, but what everybody does not realize is the enormous advantage to be gained from a thorough initial preparation. There should be no difficulty about that, in these days when nearly every gardener is his own compost-maker.

The Arbutus

The Arbutus or Strawberry tree is not very often seen in these islands, except in south-west Eire, where it grows wild, but is an attractive evergreen of manageable size and accommodating disposition. True, most varieties object to lime, belonging as they do to the family of *Ericaceae*, like the heaths and the rhododendrons, but the one called *Arbutus Unedo* can safely be planted in any reasonable soil.

To enumerate its virtues. It is, as I have said, evergreen. It will withstand sea-gales, being tough and woody. It has an amusing, shaggy, reddish bark. It can be grown in the open as a shrub, or trained against a wall, which perhaps shows off the bark to its fullest advantage, especially if you can place it where the setting sun will strike on it, as on the trunk of a Scots pine. Its waxy, pinkish-white flowers, hanging like clusters of tiny bells among the dark green foliage, are useful for picking until the first frost of November browns them; a drawback which can be obviated by a hurried picking when frost threatens. And to my mind, its greatest charm is that it bears flower and fruit at the same time, so that you get the strawberry-like berries dangling red beneath the pale flowers. These berries are edible, but I do not recommend them. According to Pliny, who confused it with the real strawberry, the word *unedo*, from *unum edo*, means 'I eat one', thus indicating that you don't come back for more.

After its virtues, it only fault: it is not quite hardy enough for very cold districts, or for the North.

There is another arbutus called *Menziesii*, which is the noble Madrona tree of California, reaching a height of 100 feet and more in its native home. I doubt if it would ever reach that height in England, though I must admit that the one I planted here in Kent some fifteen years ago is growing with alarming rapidity and has already obscured a ground-floor window; soon it will have attained the next floor, and what do I do then? Let it grow as high as the roof, I suppose, and beyond. Its lovely bark – mahogany colour until it starts to peel, revealing an equally lovely olive green underneath – gives me such pleasure that I could never bear to cut it down. Perhaps an exceptionally severe winter will deal with the problem, for it is marked with the dagger of warning, meaning 'tender' in the catalogues.

There is also *Arbutus Andrachne*, with the characteristic red bark, but this, again, is suitable only for favoured regions such as south and south-west England, parts of Wales, Northern Ireland, and south-west Eire. On the whole it is safer to stick to *Arbutus Unedo*, so rewarding with its green leaves through the winter, and so pretty with its waxy racemes and scarlet fruits in autumn.

Lily of the valley

This is a good time to plant the outdoor lily of the valley. A neighbour of mine, who has wide drifts of them among the azaleas and primulas of his beautiful woodland garden, says that he never *plants* them at all, but just throws them down on the surface with a very light covering of leaf-mould, and leaves them to find their own way down into the ground. I have not tried it, but the method certainly works well with him, probably because he has a soft rich spongy soil, intersected by little streams and offering small resistance to the roots as they feel their way about. They have queer habits; I tried to grow them under trees, which is their natural condition, but they seem to prefer coming up in the middle of a stony path. Plants are really most unpredictable.

The ordinary old English lily of the valley has the sweetest scent of all, but the large-flowered variety called Fortin's Giant has its value, because it flowers rather later and thus prolongs the season by about a fortnight.

A November tuzzy-muzzy

It is amusing and also useful as a record of what to plant *now*, looking forward to twelve months hence, to make a compact little bunch of what may be found flowering out of doors in this drear empty month. Prowling round through the drizzle with knife and secateurs, I collected quite a presentable tuzzy-muzzy. Some bits were scented; some were merely pretty; and few of them had been grown with a special view to picking in November.

Among the scented bits were *Viburnum bodnantense* and *Viburnum fragrans*; some sprigs of *Daphne retusa*; a few stray roses, notably the Scots *Stanwell Perpetual* and the hybrid musk *Penelope* who goes on and on, untiringly, and whose every bud opens in water. To these I added some lemon-scented verbena and some ivy-leaved geranium; they had been growing all summer in the open and had not yet suffered from frost.

Among the scentless but more brightly coloured bits, I

still had some gentians and some cyclamen *neapolitanum*, both pink and white, coming up through their beautifully marbled leaves which, if you look carefully, are seen to be never quite the same from plant to plant. They surprise with their infinite variety, more innocently than Cleopatra surprised her Antony. Then I picked some sprays of *Abutilon megapotamicum* which has been flowering since last June and shows no sign of stopping until a bad frost hits it. It grows against a south wall and is given some protection in winter, not very much protection, just a heap of coarse ashes over its roots and a curtain of hessian or sacking drawn across it when the weather becomes very severe. I found some fine heads of polyanthus, entirely out of season, the blue Californian variety and some of the butter-and-cream Munstead, raised by Miss Gertrude Jekyll, that grand gardener to whom we owe so much. That was not a bad little bunch from out-of-doors, but anyone with a slightly heated greenhouse, say 45 degrees to 50 degrees, can count on a succession of flowers from a few pots of *Cypripedium insigne*, the most easily grown of all orchids, the Lady's Slipper type, with the big pouch and the wing-like petals. I cannot imagine a better Christmas present than a well-filled pot, for the flower has an astonishing faculty for lasting several weeks either on the plant or picked for a vase, and the plant itself will survive for many years. I don't believe that a greenhouse would be necessary: a window-sill in a room where the temperature never dropped below 45 degrees should suffice. They do not like very strong sunlight, and they do like plenty of water.

They need re-potting every three years or so, and it is best to get a ready-made mixture from a nurseryman. Re-plant as firmly as you possibly can, ramming the sphagnum compost down with strong fingers and a blunt stick like an enormously fat, unsharpened pencil, and use plenty of small crocks for drainage.

Poplars

It often surprises me that we in Britain do not plant poplars more extensively. Whether grown as single sentinels or in a long regimental row, it seems to me that they fit as suitably into the southern English landscape as the cypress into the landscape of Italy; and for the northern counties as for Scotland, the silvery aspen, *Populus tremula*, which, anyway, is happier up there than in a softer climate, adds a coolness appropriately Nordic.

There is surely much to be said in favour of the poplar. First, it grows so rapidly that if you are out for a quick return on your money you can get it within twelve to fifteen years. (Landlords and farmers please note.) If it is not money you are after, you will have the gratification of supplying some extra beauty to the countryside; and that still means something to some of us, even if we must be counted in a dwindling minority. Secondly, the poplar will grow and thrive, enjoying itself, in wet ground which no hardwood tree such as the oak or beech would have a favourable word to say for. Thirdly, you can get it for nothing. I know it enrages my good friends the nurserymen when I say this; but I do have to consider my more impecunious readers, and so will say boldly that if you thrust a twig or even a big wrist-thick bit of poplar into the ground and stamp it in very tight, it will take root and grow within four or five years into something that already begins to look like a tree. This is the time of year to do it; November, when the leaves have dropped.

There are several different sorts of poplar. There is the

Black poplar, *Populus nigra*, which, in this country, we generally call the Lombardy poplar, that tall, towering, pointed tree, the most familiar one, but all too rare in our landscape. Then there is the Balsam poplar, which smells so good and resinous on a spring breeze, suddenly; a spreading-out tree, not so elegantly shapely as the Lombardy, but with the advantage of the leaf scenting the air, very exciting when you catch it.

A word of warning. Do not plant poplars where their roots can interfere with the foundations of your house or with drains or land-drains or anything else that their roots are liable to heave up. Poplars may make lines of gold overhead, but their root-system can be very mischievous underneath.

Late autumn foliage

The red leaves have nearly all gone by late November. The *Liquidambar* still retains some, in a variegation of red-and-green; they cling on for so long that they might be glued on. What an amazing sight this tree must be, in its native home of the eastern United States, where it can grow to a height of 150 ft. It must be alarming to come upon, like a giant torch one ought to extinguish, lest it set fire to a whole forest. It was introduced into this country so far back as 1683, but has never yet attained a comparable height here, and may confidently be planted as a sort of exclamation mark of autumn's dying farewell, for it grows upright and pointed, like a poplar.

From the shape of its leaf, it might easily be mistaken for a maple, which it is not. I have no great liking for the Japanese maple, *Acer palmatum*, commonly seen, though seldom seen at its best, but there is a Chinese maple which

I dearly love, partly for its beautiful orange-brown bark, and chiefly for the autumn colour which it holds so long. This is *Acer griseum* which will eventually grow to 40 ft. in height, but which even in youth makes a most lovely little tree, like a tree in a fairy story, light and delicate, and bronze as the party-shoes of one's childhood.

Both of these I grow, and have been long acquainted with, but I must confess with shame that the red chokeberry was unfamiliar until someone recently brought me a branch. It flamed as red as a cherry. I think it probably ought to be planted in a clump, say half a dozen, for it makes only a little bushy shrub, 5 to 8 ft. high, and a single specimen might not do it justice. Of course the snag about all trees or shrubs deliberately planted for autumn colour in a country garden is that they are apt to merge with the trees of the woodland or the hedgerows beyond, in rivalry with the beech, the wild cherry, the Service tree, and even the oaks, but a concentration in a chosen corner will always indicate that they have been put there on purpose.

There are three kinds of chokeberry, and all three are said to colour well; their botanical names are *Aronia arbutifolia*, which is the one I saw; *A. melanocarpa*, the black chokeberry, with white flowers and blackish fruits; and *A. prunifolia*.

An idea from France

One does not, in the southern provinces of France, pick up many ideas for northern gardens; the climate is too different, not only because many desirable plants would not be hardy with us, but also because the strong sunshine beautifies groups of colour which at home would look only too like the bedding-out of a municipal garden. Scarlet salvia, cannas, and even begonias glow with an intensity that gives them a new character.

I did, however, note a way of using one very ordinary plant, which at first sight I took to be our old friend the Virginia creeper, *Ampelopsis Veitchii*. I have always thought it a potentially very handsome thing in itself, as sanguine in autumn as any maple, but not when we behold it glued against the wall of a red brick villa. Here in the south I saw it growing free, tumbling in cascades over some terrace or clambering through some dark green tree, to fall back in long loose strands of scarlet. Given its liberty it is as startling as the red *tropaeolum* which ramps in Scotland, but is often recalcitrant in England. I can imagine it wreathing a holly, or hanging amongst the branches of an ilex (holm-oak) if you are so fortunate as to possess a fully grown one, or even scrambling along a rough hedge of thorn. Very often one finds such hedges with a holly left to grow high, I believe because country people retain an old superstition that it is unlucky to cut holly down to hedge-level. However that may be, the sudden pryamid of scarlet and green would flare like a torch, especially when caught by the low rays of an autumnal sun.

I have laid emphasis on the advantage of some dark tree as a host for the creeper, because to my mind the combination of dark green and brilliant red is one of the most effective in nature, but I do recall once seeing a Virginia creeper that had found its way high into the branches of a silver birch. There it hung, pale pink and transparent in the delicacy of the white tree. It must have been a garden escape, for no one would have thought of planting it there, on the edge of a wood.

The same idea could be extended to some of the ornamental vines, *Vitis coignetiae* for example, or *Vitis vinifera Brandt*. These have on the whole received better treatment than the Virginia creeper. Not adhesive or self-clinging, they have mostly been used over pergolas or archways, when their beautiful rosy leaves could dangle at their will, receiving the maximum of luminous light that they crave and deserve. Not enough use is made of ornamental vines in this country, nor have we learnt to grow them in the way they can best be used, as I could imagine them pouring loose and unrestricted, as I saw them treated, all careless and rampant over the terraces and parapets of ruined castle walls in my beloved corner of south western France.

More about the small garden

The problem of the small garden. I received a letter which went straight to my heart, more especially as it contained a plaintive cry that unintentionally scanned as a line of verse, 'I never shall adapt my means to my desires.' A perfectly good alexandrine, concisely expressing the feelings of millions if not of millionaires.

The writer has a back garden 50 by 35 ft., and a front garden which he dismisses as being like any small villa in extent. How, he asks, would I harden my own heart if I had to decide between the demands of priority for the different seasons? Would I drop out one of the flowering periods altogether? No, I would not. I should always want at least one winter-flowering shrub. Wych-hazel for choice, and at least one tree of the cherry, *Prunus subhirtella autumnalis*, giving branches to pick from November till March, and the yellow winter jasmine against a back wall of the house. Much use can be made of house-walls for climbers, without robbing any space from the garden proper.

I should have little narrow beds running round three sides of the house, south, east and west, and these I should fill with bulbs of various kinds, dependent upon the taste of the owner: and dependent also upon the requirements of the bulbs, keeping the sun-loving kinds to the south, and kinds more tolerant of shade, such as snowdrops and winter aconites, to the east and west. I should cram my southerly bed with anemones, all opening to the sun, the blue Greek anemone *blanda*, the Italian blue *apennina*, and with the exquisite anemone *St. Bavo*, insufficiently grown yet so easy and self-sowing, of a beauty that far transcends the coarser blooms of *Anemone St. Brigid* or even the handsome *Anemone de Caen*. These narrow beds I should overplant with a variety of low-growing things, again dependent upon their choice of aspect, perhaps the creeping thymes to the south, making a red and lilac carpet of flower in late May and early June, perhaps the smaller violets to the east and west, but I should also leave spaces between them for the sowing of some chosen annuals, the blue *cynoglossum* and *phacelia*, also the Cambridge blue lobelia, and any other dwarf annuals as taste may dictate. These would make a summer display when the bulbs had died down, and would even persist into autumn if late sowings were made. On the north side, I would have foxgloves, of which many improved varieties are now obtainable.

This leaves the centre of the plot free for any bed or side border in which to grow flowering shrubs or herbaceous perennials. The boundary hedges I should unquestionably make of some flowering subject, since the wish of my correspondent is to prolong his season as far as possible. Some roses make an extremely effective hedge, the old striped *Rosa mundi*, for instance, or *conditorum*, more prettily known as *Assemblage des Beautés*; and there are evergreen kinds of berberis, flowering in spring and fruiting in autumn. It should thus be feasible, in the smallest plot, to cover the year and with ingenuity to do even better than I have suggested, by filling every odd corner with things like the September-October colchicums, the little pink and white cyclamen, too lowly to get in anybody's way, and some blue splashes of gentian if the soil is suitable.

The snowflake

I don't think we grow the snowflake or *Leucojum* nearly enough. It is so graceful, being much taller than the snowdrop, its dangling bells rising 18 in. high through its rush-like leaves in April. May God forgive me, in my younger days I dug up a whole colony in a derelict garden I was trying to reedem; I didn't appreciate their beauty and recklessly moved them to an out-of-the-way corner where I am glad to say a few still survive. It was a particularly fine sample, in spite of being wickedly over-crowded, and should have been divided years before I ever came on it at all. These are the shocking things one does when one knows no better.

I know a bit better now, and would not be without *Leucojum aestivum*, especially the variety known as Gravetye. It flowers in April or May, which is rather misleading since *aestivum* means summer. *Leucojum vernum* is more true to its adjective, since it really flowers in spring: even as early as February or March, and is a very pretty thing for the rock-garden or for naturalizing in grass. It is a most obliging plant, since it will thrive either in sun or shade, and does not mind a limy soil. Like the snowdrop, it should be dug up and divided and replanted as soon as the flower begins to fade. This seems rather a strange thing to do, when

221

we are always told to let foliage of bulbs turn yellow and die down before attempting to lift the bulbs at all. Snowdrops and snowflakes work contrariwise. They like to be lifted while they are still in full green leaf, broken up, and reassembled in new young clumps.

Leucojum autumnale is rather a spindly-looking thing, lacking the solidity of *vernum* and *aestivum*. It is said to be hardy, but personally I do not feel tempted to bother about it; one has these prejudices, and must abide by them. I do, however, very strongly recommend the spring and so-called summer snowflakes, which gives a good return for your money in their yearly increase, as may be said of most bulbs.

Unsuitable soils

Will I please write about Lime-haters or What not to waste Time on? My resolve to comply with this request has been strengthened by a lament from a gentleman who bought a *Pieris Forrestii* last spring, planted it very carefully in the chalk of Epsom Downs, and is now surprised to find it showing every sign of imminent collapse.

It is not possible to lay down any absolute and comprehensive law. There are some border-line plants which, although happier on an acid (lime-free) soil, will still put up with a certain degree of alkalinity. It is generally known, I suppose, that most members of the vast Natural Order of *Ericaceae* are hostile to lime, thus imposing a serious limitation on people who wish to grow rhododendrons, camellias, azaleas, kalmias, andromedas, pernettyas, vacciniums, and the majority of heaths and heathers; though even this large family includes some members willing to oblige, *Rhododendron hirsutum* and *Rhododendron racemosum*, for example, and *Erica carnea* among the heaths.

So no one need wholly despair. But at the same time my first bit of advice to people determined to attempt things reluctant to thrive on an unsuitable soil would be: Don't. It is much better to stick to the things that happen to like the kind of soil you have got in your garden and give other things a miss. I know this is a hard saying, cutting out a whole lot of temptations, but I am sure it is a right one. It is no good trying to force plants to adopt a way of life they don't like: they just won't have it, unless you are rich enough to undertake excavations the size of a quarry. My second bit of advice would be: Make quite sure what type of soil you possess. There are various methods by which the amateur can make a test for himself, but only a rough estimate can be arrived at, and it is much better to bother a professional chemist. Any horticultural college or your county horticultural adviser will carry out the necessary test. If the sample is found to be acid or neutral, well and good: if it is found to be limy, you will have to proceed on a system of cautious elimination. There is a mysterious formula known as the pH scale: pH five and six are entirely acid and are the best for all working purposes; pH seven is neutral; and anything above pH seven is alkaline, or limy, and must therefore be regarded with suspicion.

December

Winter flowers for cutting

I find, and do not doubt that most people will agree with me, that November and December are quite the bleakest months of the year for finding 'something to pick for indoors.' A flowerless room is a soul-less room, to my thinking; but even one solitary little vase of a living flower may redeem it. So in this note I propose to suggest some things that everybody can grow with a prophetic eye on next winter so that the usual blank period may not occur again. These will be things that flourish out of doors. I am not here concerned with greenhouses.

Viburnum fragrans will start producing its apple-blossom flowers in November, and unless interrupted by a particularly severe frost will carry on until March. It is a shrub growing eventually to a height of ten or twelve feet; it is extremely hardy; easy-going as to soil; and has the merit of producing a whole nursery of children in the shape of young self-rooted shoots. Picked and brought into a warm room, it is very sweet scented.

The Christmas roses, *Helleborus niger*, are in flower now. They don't like being moved – in gardening language, they 'resent disturbance' – so even if you will take my advice and plant some clumps in early spring, which is the best time to move them, directly after they have finished flowering, you may have to wait a year or two before they begin to reward you with their greenish-white flowers and their golden centres. They are worth waiting for, believe me.

They like a rather shady place; moist, but well drained. A western aspect suits them. Once planted, leave them alone. They will grow in strength from year to year. I have a plant in my garden which to my certain knowledge has been there for fifty years. It was bequeathed to me by an old country-woman of the old type, who wanted me to have the enjoyment of it after she had gone.

Hamamelis mollis. This is the wych-hazel, a small tree which begins to flower on its bare branches in January. It is a real tough, which will grow anywhere – any soil, any aspect – though the better you treat it the better it will do. This applies to most plants, as to most people. The wych-hazel will give you scented twigs for picking at a very early age.

Then there is *Prunus subhirtella autumnalis*. This is a little tree which, as its name suggests, ought to flower in autumn. As a matter of fact, in this country it flowers in November or December, and is very useful on that account. Pick it in the bud; bring it indoors; and it will open into a fountain of bridal-looking blossom. It is said to strike very easily from cuttings taken in early summer from the current year's growth. I prefer it grown as a bush, not as a standard.

I should like to put in one last word for that very common plant, the pink-flowering currant, *Ribes sanguineum*. Nothing could be easier to grow, and it is sometimes despised on that account; but those who have the wit to cut some long stems of it in January, and to keep them in water in a dark cupboard, and to bring them out into the light in March, will find not pink but a snow-white sheaf, a bride's sheaf, to reward them.

Herbs for the kitchen

We are now in process of restoring a small herb garden after years of war neglect. During the war years we managed to keep a table-cloth-sized herb-garden going, just outside the kitchen door: a few chives, a solitary plant of lovage, some thyme, some apple-mint, and a clump of garlic. This meant that the wise cook could dash out of the kitchen and quickly grab a handful of something that would turn the salad or the sandwiches into something that made guests ask them what on earth had been put into them.

My answer to this was always, simply and monosyllabically, 'Herbs.' Why don't English women use more herbs in their concoctions? They are easy to grow: take up little room, and make all the difference. *Lovage*, with its leaves finely shredded, will convert a dull lettuce into a salad worthy of a good French restaurant. *Chervil* will serve the same good purpose, and has the additional attraction of meaning 'the leaf that rejoices the heart.' It can be made to rejoice the heart also in soups and stews. *Chives*, those little brothers of the onion, are so accommodating that they can be grown even in a window-box in a city. *Tarragon* can be used for the omelette and the eggs; and if you put a leaf of it into a bottle of vinegar the vinegar will greatly benefit.

Pinks

At this great planting season of the year we should do well to consider the vast tribe of Pinks, or *Dianthus*, for there are few plants more charming, traditional, or accommodating. In old kitchen gardens one used to see long strips of *Mrs. Sinkins* bordering the paths, and what could be more desirable than that ragged old lady heavily scenting the air? She is a very old lady indeed. Some people think she may be as much as 140 years old, though others would make her a mere 80 or so: and say that she had her origin in a workhouse garden at Slough. Whatever the truth about Mrs. Sinkins may be, she appears proudly on the armorial bearings of the borough of Slough, firmly held in the beak of a swan.

She has a daughter, *Miss Sinkins*, less well known, but tidier and more prim in her habits, a retiring Victorian maiden whom you are unlikely to find in a search through most nurserymen's catalogues. In all the pile of catalogues on my table I can find only one nurseryman who lists her; and he tells me that his stock is small, although he hopes to raise a larger supply next year. Do not worry about this, for there are plenty of the family to choose from. Our native Cheddar Pink, *Dianthus caesius*, is almost as heavily scented as *Mrs. Sinkins* herself, and is as easy to grow.

This applies to nearly all the pinks. They make few demands. Sun-lovers, they like a well-drained and rather gritty soil; and if you can plant them with a generous supply of mortar rubble they will be as happy as the years are long. This means, of course, that they prefer growing in lime or chalk, an alkaline soil; but they don't insist on it; they exact so little that they will put up with almost anything except a waterlogged place. They hate that; and will revenge themselves on you by damping off.

The only other fault they have, a most endearing fault, revealing an all too generous nature, is that they may flower themselves to death in your service. You must be on the look-out for this, and cut the wealth of flowers hard back to the grey-green clumps, to protect and save them from their own extravagant generosity.

Companions for roses

A lady writes to ask what she can grow as an edging to her rose-beds. She wants something out of the ordinary, something that will flower all the summer, something that will require no attention, and, of course, it must be a perennial. Is that, she says, asking too much?

This inquiry rather put me on my mettle. I did not dare to suggest anything so obvious as catmint (*Nepeta Mussinii*) which would have fulfilled all her demands with the single proviso that by way of 'attention' she would have to cut it right back to the base in early spring. Clearly, it is difficult to find something that will at least look neat when not in flower. The rock-roses perhaps provide as long a flowering period as anything, but there again you would have to clip them back after their first rush of bloom (which does last for at least two months) in order to make them break out again later on, and this operation might also come under the heading of 'attention.' The Cheddar Pink, *Dianthus caesius*, I thought, would look neat and gay as an edging, with the additional charm of the exceedingly sweet smell from its masses of pale rosy flowers. Two little speedwells, *Veronica repens* and *Veronica rupestris*, would be pretty in their mats of china blue; and the rather taller *Veronica incana*, with darker blue spikes, would offer the advantage of tidy silvery leaves. *Gypsophila fratensis* and *Tunica saxifraga* would both trail in a foam of pink, like small clouds touched by sunset. Or, if my correspondent desired a strong colour, the low-growing *Viola Huntercombe purple*, most intense and imperial, would glow in a manner to attract notice even from a distance. Or, if she desired no colour at all, the beautifully shaped *Viola septentrionalis*, pure white, with leaves like a violet.

But, I added in my reply to my correspondent, why restrict your rosebuds to a mere edging? Why not allow the plants to encroach all over the beds? It will do the roses no harm, in fact it will supply a living mulch to keep the ground moist and the roses cool at the roots. It was, I think, that great gardener William Robinson who first advocated and practised this revolutionary idea. His roses certainly throve in spite of, or because of, it. When one murmured something about manure, he snorted and said that it was quite unnecessary. I fancy, however, that in these days of compost heaps he would have agreed to some generous handfuls being inserted as a top-dressing annually between the plants; or even some organic fertilizer such as bonemeal.

Colour in December

It is pleasant to see the garden laid to bed for the winter. Brown blankets of earth cover the secret roots. Nothing is seen overground, but a lot is going on underneath in preparation for the spring. It is a good plan, I think, to leave a heavy mulch of fallen leaves over the flowering shrubs instead of sweeping them all away. They serve the double purpose of providing protection against frost, and of eventually rotting down into the valuable humus that all plants need. There are leaves and leaves, of course, and not all of them will rot as quickly as others. Oak and beech are the best: to compose into leaf mould in a large square pile; but any leaves will serve as a mulch over beds and borders throughout the hard months to come.

The professional gardener will raise objections. He will tell you that the leaves will 'blow all over the place' as soon as a wind gets up. This is true up to a point, but can be prevented by a light scattering of soil or sand over the leaves to hold them down. This sort of objection may often be overcome by the application of some common sense. There are few people more obstinate than the professional or jobbing gardener. Stuck in his ideas, he won't budge.

November and December make a difficult blank time for the gardener. One has to fall back on the berrying plants; and amongst these I would like to recommend the seldom-grown *Celastrus orbiculatus*. This is a rampant climber, which will writhe itself up into any old valueless fruit tree, apple or pear, or over the roof of a shed, or over any space not wanted for anything more choice. It is rather a dull green plant during the summer months; you would not notice it then at all; but in the autumn months of October and November it produces its butter-yellow berries which presently break open to show the orange seeds, garish as heraldry, *gules* and *or*, startling to pick for indoors when set in trails against dark wood panelling, but equally lovely against a white-painted wall.

It is a twisting thing. It wriggles itself into corkscrews, not to be disentangled, but this does not matter because it never needs pruning unless you want to keep it under control. My only need has been to haul it down from a tree into which it was growing too vigorously; a young prunus, which would soon have been smothered. Planted at the foot of an old dead or dying tree, it can be left to find its way upwards and hang down in beaded swags, rich for indoor picking, like thousands of tiny hunter's moons coming up over the eastern horizon on a frosty night.

The earliest flowers

I know someone who averts his eyes from all young growth, such as narcissus leaves pushing through, prior to

January 1st, but who, after that date, peers eagerly in the hope of even a rare snowdrop. We know full well that January and February can be the most unpleasant months in the calendar, but they do bring some consolation in the beginnings of revival. Crocuses and other small bulbs appear, miraculous and welcome; they are apt, however, to leave a blank after they have died down, and it is for that reason that I suggest overplanting them with some little shrubs which will flower in February or March.

I visualize a low bank or slope of ground, not necessarily more than two or three feet high, perhaps bordering some rough steps on a curve. You stuff and cram the bank with early-flowering bulbs, making a gay chintz-like or porcelain effect with their bright colours in yellow, blue, white, orange, red. Amongst these, you plant the little shrubs I want to recommend, *Corylopsis spicata* and *Corylopsis pauciflora* are two of the prettiest and softest, hung with yellow moths of flowers all along their twiggy branches. They are natives of Japan, and are related to the wych-hazels. They seldom grow more than four feet high and about as much through; they need no pruning, and are graceful in their growth, pale as a primrose, and as early. Another little companion shrub on the bank would be *Forsythia ovata*. The big bushy forsythia is well known, but this small relation from Korea is not so often seen. It is perfectly hardy, and makes a tiny tree three to four feet high, flowering into the familiar golden blossoms, a golden rain pouring down in companionship with the *Corylopsis*, after the bulbs have died away.

There is also a dwarf variety of the favourite *Viburnum fragrans*, called *compactum*, which would associate happily.

If you have room in your garden at the top of the bank

or slope, I would urge you to plant *Cornus mas*, the Cornelian cherry. This cornel or dog-wood produces its yellow flowers in February, and is one of the best winter flowerers for picking for indoors. A big full-grown tree of *Cornus mas* is a sight to be seen, as I once saw one growing in a wood in *Kent*. It towered up fifteen feet and more, smothered in its myriads of tiny clusters, each individual flower-head like a bunch of snipped ribbons. If at first it seems a little disappointing and makes only a thin show, do not be discouraged, for it improves yearly with age and size, and one year will suddenly surprise you by the wealth of its blossom. It also produces long scarlet berries which you can, if you wish, eat.

An early flowering shrub

I have mentioned, amongst early flowering shrubs, *Corylopsis pauciflora*. The Corylopsis is a little shrub, not more than four or five feet high and about the same in width, gracefully hung with pale yellow flowers along the leafless twigs, March to April, a darling of prettiness. *Corylopsis spicata* is much the same, but grows rather taller, up to six feet, and is, if anything more frost-resistant. They are not particular as to soil, but they do like a sheltered position, if you can give it to them, say with a backing of other wind-breaking shrubs against the prevailing wind.

Sparrows. . . . They peck the buds off, so put a bit of old fruit-netting over the plant in October or November when the buds are forming. Sparrows are doing the same to my Winter-sweet this year, as never before; sheer mischief; an avian form of juvenile delinquency; so take the hint and protect the buds with netting before it is too late.

Abutilon

Abutilon megapotamicum bears no resemblance at all to the hollyhocks as we know them in cottage gardens. It is a thing to train up against a sunny south wall, and if you should happen to have a whitewashed wall or even a wall of grey stone, it will show up to special advantage against it. It has long pointed leaves and curiously shaped flowers, dark red and yellow, somewhat like a fuchsia, hanging from flexible, limp, graceful sprays. It is on the tender side, not liking too many degrees of frost, so should be covered over in winter. But perhaps you know all this already.

The idea I wanted to put forward is something that occurred to me accidentally, as gardening ideas do sometimes occur to one. I thought how pretty it might be to train an Abutilon as a standard. You see, it could be persuaded to weep downwards, like a weeping willow or a weeping cherry, if you grew it up on a short stem and constantly trimmed off all the side shoots it tried to make, till you got a big rounded head pouring downwards like a fountain dripping with the red and yellow flowers for months and months and months throughout the summer.

The Christmas rose

This seems a good occasion to mention the Christmas rose, *Helleborus niger*, in high Dutch called Christ's herb, 'because it flowereth about the birth of our Lord.' Its white flowers are, or should be, already on our tables. There is a variety called *altifolius*, which is considered superior, owing to its longer stalks; but it is often stained with a somewhat dirty pink, and I think the pure white is far lovelier. Christmas roses like a rather moist, semi-shady place in rich soil, though they have no objection to lime; they do not relish disturbance, but if you decide to plant some clumps you should do so as soon as they have finished flowering, which is another good reason for mentioning them now. If you already have old-established clumps, feed them well in February with a top dressing of compost or rotted manure, or even a watering of liquid manure, and never let them get too dry in summer. It is perhaps superfluous to say that they should be protected by a cloche when the buds begin to open, not because they are not hardy but because the low-growing flowers get splashed and spoilt by rain and bouncing mud.

The Christmas rose, although not a native of Britain, has been for centuries in our gardens. Spenser refers to it in the *Faerie Queene*, and it is described as early as 1597 in his *Herball* by John Gerard, who considered that a purgation of hellebore was 'good for mad and furious men.' Such a decoction might still come in useful today. Perhaps Gerard was quoting Epictetus, who, writing in the first century A.D., remarks that the more firmly deluded is a madman, the more hellebore he needs. Unfortunately, this serviceable plant is not very cheap to buy, but it is a very good investment because, to my positive knowledge, it will endure and even increase in strength for fifty years and more. It is also possible, and not difficult, to grow it from seed, but if you want to do that you should make sure of getting freshly ripened seed, otherwise you may despair of germination after twelve months have gone by and will crossly throw away a pan of perfectly viable seeds which only demanded a little more patience.

Winter vases

What a difficult time it is to produce flowers to fill even a few vases in the house! The winter-flowering cherry, *Prunus subhirtella autumnalis*, is a great stand-by. I have been cutting small branches of it for two weeks past, standing them in water in a warm room, when the green buds surprisingly expand into the white, faintly-scented blossom suggestive of spring. This is a little tree which should be planted in every garden. It doesn't take up much space, and pays a rich dividend for picking from November until March. Even if frost catches some of the buds, it seems able, valiant little thing that it is, to create a fresh supply.

Then there is *Mahonia japonica*, var. *Bealei*, a prickly berberis-like shrub which throws up spikes of pale lemon-coloured flower, scented like lily-of-the-valley. It is not a remarkably pretty plant, not a plant to grow for its beauty, only for the sake of the flower it will give in this dead season, so I would advise sticking it into any spare corner, with a little shelter from other shrubs if possible. It will do well in any ordinary decent soil, and it doesn't mind a bit of shade. You may have met it under the name *Berberis Bealei*.

Those are both out-of-door plants, to be grown in anybody's garden. For somebody who has got a greenhouse, slightly heated up to 40 or 50 degrees, just enough to keep the frost out, I would like to recommend the Lady Slipper Orchid, *Cypripedium insigne*. This really is a worth-while thing to grow as a pot plant. The flowers, when you cut them, will last for nearly six weeks indoors; possibly not quite so long in a grimy city, but certainly in a clean atmosphere. The type is greenish, with a brown pouch lined with yellow, and there are many attractive hybrids in variations of colour. It is a most obliging creature, practically indestructible provided you don't let it get frost-bitten or forget to give it water. It will probably need repotting every three or four years, in a sphagnum compost which is best bought ready-mixed from a nurseryman.

Shrubs in winter

Quite an attractive woody little shrub is *Callicarpa Giraldii*. It is perhaps not wildly exciting, but it makes a change from the more usual barberries and cotoneasters and gives some colour in November and December, also looks pretty in a glass under an electric lamp. The flowers, which come earlier in the year, are inconspicuous; the point is the deep-mauve berry, growing close to the stem in clusters, about the size of those tiny sugar-coated sweets which children called Hundreds and Thousands. I doubt if it would be hardy enough for very bleak or northern districts, though it should do well in a sunny corner in a line south of the Wash, as the weather reports say; it came undamaged through 18 degrees of frost in my garden last winter.

There is one vital thing to remember about *Callicarpa*: it is one of those sociable plants which like company of their own kind, so you must put at least two or three in a clump together, otherwise you won't get the berries. It is not a question of male and female plants, as, for example, with the Sea Buckthorn, which will not give its orange fruits unless married; the explanation appears to be simply that it enjoys a party.

This, of course, is true of many of the berrying shrubs, as well as of many human beings.

I am told that it makes a pretty pot-plant, grown in a single stem, when the berries cluster even more densely, all the way up. Here, again, it would be necessary to have several pots, not only one.

Another small shrub looking very cheerful just now, is

Coronilla glauca. Puzzled, I looked it up in some books, and found that it was meant to flower from April till June. I can't help that. All I know is that it is flowering now in my own garden, and similarly in a neighbour's garden, and flowered continuously in both our gardens throughout December of last year. This record seems to establish it as a winter-flowerer. It is not deciduous, holding its grey-green leaves and carrying its bright-yellow vetch-like flowers throughout the dark days. A nice, useful gay little shrub, perhaps not hardy enough for very cold areas, but happy under a house wall in a narrow border in the south-east in Kent or Sussex and further west.

There is another form of it, which I confess I have never seen and which I therefore hesitate to recommend. This is called *Coronilla Emerus*, or the Scorpion Senna. The description tempts me. It claims to bear yellow and copper-red flowers in great profusion through June and July, and to be easy and more frost-resistant than *Coronilla glauca*. I think I shall order one of these, and see what happens.

Dwarf shrubs

How comforting it is to feel that we still have at least three months before us in which to plant the shrubs we had forgotten. These after-thoughts can safely go in at any time up to next March, in fact most evergreens prefer to wait until the soil is likely to start warming up. This reflection gives us a sense of respite and reprieve.

One of the most charming small shrubs for the rock garden is *Syringa Palibiniana*. I do resent having to call a thing syringa when what I really mean is lilac, but I cannot go against the dictum of my betters. *Syringa Palibiniana*, from Korea, resembles what we should consider a miniature

237

lilac, and the great point about it is its remarkable fragrance. Bury your face in its neat rounded top in May if you want to get all the distilled scent of every dew-drenched lilac you ever smelt. It comes high in the list of my garden darlings.

Perhaps I ought to qualify the term small or miniature shrub, since this is likely to lead to confusion. Most nurserymen who list it claim that it grows only to 3 ft. high. This is wrong: since in fact it will eventually grow to about 8 ft., a very different matter. Reputable nurserymen do not deliberately mislead their customers; leaving integrity apart, it would not pay them to do so. I think what has happened in the case of this syringa is that it starts to flower so profusely and at so young an age that a dwarf habit has been too rashly assumed.

What, then, are we to do? Obviously, we can't burden a small rock-garden with a shrub that intends to grow far taller than its companions or even than ourselves. There seems to be only one answer: plant it, enjoy it while it remains pigmy enough to share its place amongst other Lilliputians; and then when it gets above itself, dig it up and replant it in some open place where it can grow away to its Korean heart's content and let us see what happens.

I have, for the time being, put it amongst some daphnes of a similar round-headed type, Daphne *retusa* and *collina*, and have inter-planted them with a handful of the pink-and-white striped tulip *Clusiana*, the Lady-tulip. They should look pretty together, if only my scheme comes off. Alas, how seldom do these little schemes come off. Something will go wrong; some puppy will bury a bone; some mouse will eat the bulbs; some mole will heave the daphnes and the lilac out of the ground.

Still, no gardener would be a gardener if he did not live in hope.

Protecting pot-plants in winter

Frost jumps suddenly upon us, and takes us unaware. We should not be unaware; we ought to know our climate well enough by now to be only too well aware of the dangers that may leap upon us between a sunset and a dawn. Yet how many gardeners take this threat in time? How many cover up their tender plants before it is too late?

I believe in shutting the stable door long before the horse has had a chance to get out.

These remarks may apply especially to the treatment of shrubs or plants in large pots or wooden tubs. Many people grow hydrangeas or fuchsias in tubs, and are puzzled to know what to do about them through the horrible months we have ahead of us. Common sense tells us not to water them; water would simply congeal the soil into a block as hard as concrete. A far better plan is to wrap the pots round with any warm covering you can get, straw or bracken; or if your pots are not too large, sink them into a bed of ashes up to the rim. That will prevent the frost from getting at them, for of course, you realize that a plant in a pot is far more vulnerable to frost than a plant in the ground. It has none of the protection of the deep surrounding earth, and must be artificially supplied by us with a deep, ashy sinking.

For the rest, what should one do for one's plants in pots? They are usually the most precious and treasured things. It is too large a subject to treat in so short an article, but generally speaking I would say this:

Repot any plant which has become pot-bound. You can

239

easily determine this necessity by seeing whether its roots are coming through the hole at the bottom.

If this does not seem necessary: scrape away the top-soil and give some fresh feeding, compost or bone-meal. Plants in pots naturally exhaust the soil they are planted in, and need replenishment. They have nothing else to draw on, and must depend upon us, their owners, for the nourishment they cannot obtain for themselves. Our responsibility is great towards these beautiful imaginations of Nature, so pathetically and helplessly at our command.

Self-seeding shrubs

It is well worth while, when putting the garden to bed for the winter, to search rather carefully for any stray seedlings which may have lain concealed beneath fallen leaves and the dead stalks of herbaceous stuff. It is surprising how many shrubs will thus reproduce themselves, even at some distance from their parent. They may be only a few inches high, when found, but by next spring they should start growing into useful little plants if you lift them with their roots intact and pot them up and sink the pots in a nursery row, either in ashes, sand, or ordinary soil. The point of sinking the pots is to safeguard them from getting frozen hard, as they would be if left standing nakedly in the open.

Many of the commoner shrubs, such as the berberis, the cotoneasters, the brooms, the hypericums and the buddleias, may often come to light in quantities and are just worth preserving if only to fill a gap in future or to give away.

I have also found more unexpected things than those: thriving little children of myrtle and the sweet-scented bay; the graceful indigofera; Clerodendron of the turquoise-blue berries; *Solanum crispum*, that energetic climber; and even self sown yews which if only I had had the sense and fore-sight to regiment along a drill years ago would by now have developed into a neat clippable hedge.

This is all satisfactory enough, but there are even more exciting possibilities. There is the chance that one of these stray seedlings may turn out to be better than its parent, or at any rate different. I believe I am right in saying that *Rosa Highdownensis*, that lovely hybrid of *R. Moyesii*, appeared accidentally in Sir Frederick Stern's garden at Highdown, and that *Caryopteris clandonensis* of a deeper blue than either *Caryopteris mongholica* or *C. Mastacanthus*, was suddenly noticed by the present secretary of the R.H.S. in his own garden at Clandon. Of course, to spot these finds you have to be endowed with a certain degree of serendipity, mean-ing the faculty of 'making discoveries by accident and sagacity' of something you were not deliberately in quest of.

This faculty involves knowledge, which is what Horace Walpole meant by serendipity when he coined his peculiar word. You have to know enough to recognize the novelty when you first see it, otherwise it might escape you alto-gether. You have to ensure also that the remorseless hoe does not scrape all your seedlings away into the heap destined for the barrow-load of rubbish. Scuffle about for yourself, be-fore you let a jobbing gardener loose on beds or borders.

Over winter's hump

The shortest day has passed, and whatever nastiness of weather we may look forward to in January and February, at least we can notice that the days are getting longer. Minute by minute they lengthen out. It takes some weeks before we become aware of the change. It is imperceptible even as the growth of a child, as you watch it day by day, until the moment comes when with a start of delighted surprise we realize that we can stay out of doors in a twilight lasting for another quarter of a precious hour.

There are things to pick. Not very many. One has to scrounge round, finding a berrying branch here and there, *Celastrus orbiculatus* for instance, exploding into the red and gold of its small fruits, so decorative that I wonder why people don't plant it to scramble up old trees or along rough hedges. The Christmas roses, *Helleborus niger*, are coming into flower now, and so is the winter jasmine, the yellow one, *Jasminum nudiflorum*.

We all know this jasmine. It is one of our stand-bys in the difficult months and is also one of the plants we think we can never treat so rough as to make it fail us. I protest that that is taking an unfair advantage of a most obliging friend. Thus we are told to grow it on a wall facing north, and indeed it is one of the few plants that will give without stint even in so dismal an aspect. Try it, however, in a position looking south, and note the difference in the gratitude of its golden showers. Then, again, we are instructed to cut it back violently after it has finished flowering. Docile, I followed this advice and chopped. My jasmine, which evidently knew better, has never yet recovered from the shock. (How often I regret that plants cannot talk.) Then, again, we have been taught to regard it as a climber. I don't believe it should be considered as a climber at all; at any rate, not artificially tied up to wires against a wall. I think it should be planted to pour down in loose masses from a tripod of 6-ft.-high posts lashed together into a point at the top. Unless, of course, you happen to have a terrace with a deep retaining wall for it to hang over like a curtain, which would probably suit it better than anything.

Index

Index

245

NOTES

NOTES

NOTES

NOTES